READING THE BIBLE AS

GOD'S
OWN STORY

A Catholic Approach for

Bringing Scripture to Life

D1051823

READING THE BIBLE AS

GOD'S OWN STORY

*A Catholic Approach for
Bringing Scripture to Life*

WILLIAM S. KURZ, SJ

The Word Among Us Press
9639 Doctor Perry Road
Ijamsville, Maryland 21754
www.wordamongus.org
11 10 09 08 07   1 2 3 4 5
ISBN: 978-1-59325-101-7

Unless otherwise noted, Scripture texts used in this work are taken from the Revised Standard Version Bible: Catholic Edition, Copyright © 1965 and 1966 by the Division of Christian Education of the National Council of the Churches of Christ in the U.S.A. All rights reserved. Used with permission.

Cover design by John Hamilton Design
Cover image credit: Christ Pantocrator, 6th century (encaustic on panel) by © Monastery of Saint Catherine, Mount Sinai, Egypt/ Ancient Art and Architecture Collection Ltd./ The Bridgeman Art Library

Library of Congress Cataloging-in-Publication Data
Kurz, William S., 1939-
Reading the Bible as God's own story : a Catholic approach for bringing Scripture to life / William S. Kurz.
  p. cm.
Includes bibliographical references.
ISBN 978-1-59325-101-7 (alk. paper)
1. Bible--Reading. 2. Bible--Study and teaching--Catholic Church. 3. Irenaeus, Saint, Bishop of Lyon. 4. Athanasius, Saint, Patriarch of Alexandria, d. 373. 5. Catholic Church--Doctrines. I. Title.
BS617.K87 2007
220.088'282--dc22
                    2007007768

Contents

WHY READ SCRIPTURE AS GOD'S OWN STORY

A continuing concern among Catholic leaders, especially since the Second Vatican Council, is the failure of most ordinary Catholics to spend meaningful amounts of time reading the Bible. As a matter of fact, however, before Vatican II Catholics were often not encouraged to read Scripture at all. Although they are now being urged to read the Bible, many of them still have not received the kind of helps from Catholic biblical scholars that would enable them to know *how* to read Scripture with personal profit as God's own word to them.

It is true that many Catholic biblicists have been generous and hard working in providing institutes and courses for ordinary Catholics on how to read Scripture, as well in personally guiding Bible studies and writing materials for such studies. Many of these biblical institutes and Bible studies have been helpful. Yet considerable numbers retain such an emphasis on "academic" approaches, as well as so much focus on the original meanings and historical and cultural settings of biblical books, that many lay people who take part in these institutes or studies continue to experience the Bible more as an ancient document than as God's current word to them personally or to them as part of a church community.

Reading the Bible as God's Own Story

This book is intended as another response to the need of ordinary Catholics for help in reading the Bible spiritually and theologically as God's personal word to them as members of the church. Its title, *Reading the Bible as God's Own Story: A Catholic Approach for Bringing Scripture to Life*, suggests the approach that the book will recommend and explain. To read Scripture as God's own story is clearly different from the far more common historical approach, which reads Scripture as much as possible from the perspective of the original audience of the passage or book being read. The original audience's perspective is necessarily an ancient one, millennia old. Contemporary readers often find such old circumstances and outlooks quite unfamiliar, even irrelevant, to their current concerns.

Historical approaches necessarily and appropriately emphasize the diversity and distinctions among the many books and human authors of the Bible, as well as the original historical and cultural contexts to which the particular books responded. This is important in order to read the words and passages according to their original meanings, and to avoid uncritically reading into them later and different cultural or religious mindsets, especially the presuppositions of the readers themselves. For example, the exhortation for wives to be submissive to their husbands in Ephesians 5:24 would be less misunderstood if it were interpreted historically in the context of the customary division of labor and roles in the first-century household, than if interpreted from a nineteenth-century mindset of a husband "lording" over his wife.

Reading the Bible as *God's own story* adds to and goes

beyond strictly historical approaches by assuming that the books of the Bible are written for us as twenty-first-century Christians as much as for their original audiences. Rather than emphasize the diversity of the human authors of Scripture, reading the Bible as God's story presumes that God is the ultimate single author, who both Jews and Christians believe inspired the various human authors in their writing of the biblical books.[1] Seen this way, the various books of the Bible together make up God's comprehensive story of salvation. Accentuating the overall story of the Bible makes Scripture more relevant to contemporary readers and complements the more common focus on the particular stories of creation and individual events, as well as on the numerous characters of the Bible, which more immediately catch readers' attention.

It is especially from the early church fathers that we can learn to see in the biblical stories the overarching story of how God created the world and human beings, and then how God rescued humans after they rejected his offer of friendship in their attempts to "be like God" themselves (see Genesis 3:5). The most compelling reason why Christians can read Scripture as "God's own story" is that the turning point and climax in the biblical salvation narrative, according to St. Athanasius and many church fathers, is the incarnation of God's Son as man to save us from our sins. In the incarnate Jesus, God himself has entered the biblical story of our salvation, making it his "own story" in a quite emphatic way. To read the earlier books of the Bible without taking into consideration how they relate to the incarnation is to get only part of the story.

Because we are reminded of the pivotal biblical priority of God's incarnation by the Fathers of the Church, our Catholic ancestors in the faith, Catholic readers tend to experience this emphasis as a Catholic approach. Among all Christian denominations, the Catholic Church puts the greatest stress on learning from Catholics of earlier centuries, from the patristic times of the early fathers through the Middle Ages to today. Orthodox and Protestant scholars also frequently turn to the church fathers, especially those who flourished in the centuries before the medieval period or in the eastern provinces of Christianity. But Catholics put the most emphasis on the communion of saints and on our relationship with saints from earlier periods, who are now living with Christ in heaven.

Reading the Bible with our Catholic ancestors in the faith as God's own story brings Scripture to life, because it especially acknowledges how God has entered human history and become "God with us." With the Gospel of John, we believe that "the Word became flesh and dwelt among us." Because God's Word, or Son, now lives among us, we can experience him personally, and, consequently, "we have beheld his glory, glory as of the only Son from the Father" (John 1:14). By accentuating, along with the Fathers of the Church, the biblical narrative of creation and redemption that runs through Scripture's many books, we come to understand that everything reported in Scripture is ultimately directed toward this incarnation of God's Son and the salvation of all human beings, including ourselves, from sin, alienation, and separation from God. The Bible is not, therefore, simply a collection of stories about the past. Its accounts very much pertain to us today and to our potential for eternal happiness with God our Creator.

Seeing the Bible as Mystery

The Bible understood as God's own story, i.e., his "autobiography," can also be described as a mystery. In fact, the Bible can be compared to a mystery story, or "whodunit," in two ways.[2] A mystery story always presents us with a problem or puzzle to solve, and the fun in reading the narrative is trying to figure out and eventually finding out not only "whodunit," but also how and why. The Bible shares these elements, because it allows us to uncover the "solution" to the mystery of human salvation.

Once readers of a mystery story finish the final chapter and know the who, how, and why of the puzzle, they can no longer reread the narrative in the same way as those who have no idea how the story will end. Similarly, in the Bible, after readers know whodunit (who the messianic Savior is), they cannot reread the early sections (especially the Old Testament) in the same way as those who have not heard the definitive New Testament answer to many Old Testament questions. Catholics now know the later directions in which many of the Old Testament trajectories have developed. For example, we now read Isaiah 7:14 as it is quoted in Matthew 1:23, "'Behold, a virgin shall conceive and bear a son, and his name shall be called Emmanuel' (which means, God with us)." In Isaiah 7:14, Catholics can now see beyond the predicted son of the king of Judah at the time of the prophet Isaiah to the birth of Jesus as described in Matthew. Just as knowing the solution to a good whodunit gives us new insight into events early in the story, knowing how and why our salvation was accomplished gives us new insight into the books of the Bible. We can read a good mystery story again and again, because we enjoy going back to see how the identity, motives, and *modus operandi* were revealed. Similarly, we can come back to the Bible again and again, always hoping to discover more about how God's plan for our salvation developed and was revealed.

In addition to the elements that the Bible shares with a good whodunit, there is still another sense in which the Bible can be considered a mystery, which our title, *Reading the Bible as God's Own Story*, suggests. The story that God tells in Scripture is his revelation of himself, yet God's being so transcends our understanding that this revelation will always remain "mysterious"—that is, somewhat unknown—to us. No matter how much God reveals about himself in Scripture, he will remain utterly beyond our limited mental capacities to understand or to imagine. Therefore, to the extent of our limited human abilities, we will have to work hard—but never with complete success—to understand God's biblical self-revelation.

As we shall learn from the church fathers, from the church's creeds, and from our own reading of Scripture, the heart of the biblical mystery in this second sense—that God's story exceeds human understanding—involves at least two principal questions that are beyond our unaided human understanding, the mystery of the being of our infinite God and the mystery of evil in human history. Related to these two mysteries are the questions of who God is and what kind of God he is; how and why God created the world and humans within it as originally "very good"; what later went wrong with God's good creation and our relationship to him; and how God worked out his plan for saving and reconciling alienated humans to himself.

At one level, most ordinary people are able to grasp the basic messages of Scripture. Yet uncovering the mystery of God's existence as well as the very perplexing questions of what evil is and how it should be understood can prove far more daunting. It is especially in respect to interpreting these fundamental biblical mysteries that the early church fathers can provide us with helpful models and approaches for reading Scripture.

Early Church Fathers as Examples

From the very beginning of Christianity, church leaders were forced to articulate the correct or orthodox meaning of Scripture in order to counter misunderstandings and even deliberately falsified teachings about its message. Between A.D. 50 and A.D. 64, in the letters of St. Paul—which include the earliest New Testament writings—we see Paul in his capacities as apostle, founder, and teacher correcting misleading interpretations of Scripture and false teachings about Jesus. Around A.D. 180, St. Irenaeus found himself forced to write his *Against Heresies* to counter misuses, misinterpretations, and misquotations of Scripture in various ancient false teachings now known mostly as forms of Gnosticism.[3]

In the aftermath of the Council of Nicea (A.D. 325), the bishop of Alexandria, St. Athanasius, wrote several treatises against the Arians, heretical Christians who relied heavily on biblical interpretation to deny the divinity of Jesus. The primary form of argumentation that both Irenaeus and Athanasius used to counter the false doctrines of their times was theological interpretation of Scripture, which involved interpreting the passages that were being used to justify heretical teachings within the context of the overall biblical narrative of God's creation of the world and his salvation of the human race. From the many stories and plot lines in both Old and New Testaments of Scripture, they discerned an *overarching biblical story* of how God created the universe and the human race, and how God reconciled rebellious humans to himself by sending the Son, the Second Person of the Trinity, to become incarnate and take on human flesh and nature as both true God and true man.

Over time, they summarized this foundational biblical story line, with emphasis on its dogmatic foundations, in what they referred to as the "rule of faith." Rules of faith served as criteria for judging the adequacy of interpretations of Scripture. When false teachings presented even more grave threats to Christian teaching and dogma, ecumenical councils further summarized the heart of biblical and traditional revelation as creeds, such as the Nicene Creed. Because creeds are expressed as professions of faith (i.e., "I believe in God . . ."), it is easy to overlook the fact that significant sections of both the Apostles' and the Nicene creeds are actually constructed in narrative form.

In fact, the creeds are synopses of biblical accounts—brief narratives that both summarize God's actions as recounted in Scripture and provide a key to unlocking the significance of the biblical texts taken as a total collection. In short, from among the widely diverse biblical narratives in both Old and New Testaments, creeds provide a summary narrative of the central and essential divine story line. From among the many plot lines of Scripture, creeds select and emphasize the core stories about God's creation of the universe and human beings, about humans' rebellion against their Creator, and about God's efforts to bring humans to reconciliation. God's saving efforts culminate in the incarnation, death, and resurrection of the Son of God, the Son's establishment of and active sacramental presence within his church, and the Son's future return as judge of all.

From such early church leaders as Sts. Irenaeus and Athanasius, we can learn a good deal about how to identify and interpret the central theological messages of Scripture without getting distracted by historical details about the particular authors and audiences of the Bible's various books. In doing so, we will be using these early fathers as guides toward growing in our contemporary understanding of the mysteries about God, creation, evil, sin, and salvation that are revealed in Scripture, when we interpret it as God's word and not merely as a set of ancient human documents.

The Mystery That Is Key to Scripture

One of the most foundational biblical mysteries emphasized by the church fathers is the incarnation as man of the Son of God, the Second Person of the Trinity. Even the New Testament writers realized that the incarnation was the key to unlocking the other mysteries of Scripture (as in John 1:14, "And the Word became flesh and dwelt among us, full of grace and truth; we have beheld his glory, glory as of the only Son from the Father"). Similarly, early patristic writers treated the incarnation of the Son as true God and true man as key to understanding the entire message of Scripture. Patristic scholar Robert Louis Wilken endorses this patristic view as valid even for today, and sums it up this way:

> To learn the Lord's style of language we must begin with Christ, God's unique Word made flesh, as he is made known to us in the New Testament. For it is in him that we see

God most fully and through him that our sight is trained to interpret God's signs in creation, in history, and in the Scriptures.[4]

Irenaeus and Athanasius saw the incarnation of God's Son as man and his consequent mediation between God and the human race as the turning point in the biblical story of sin and salvation, of human alienation from and later reconciliation with God. In other words, the incarnation was their principle answer to the "whodunit" questions of the Old Testament seen as God's mystery story and so informed all other readings of Scripture.

The Bible viewed as mystery story contains many whodunit questions. There are questions about who made the universe and human beings. Because we believe that creation is good, there is the question of who or what caused all the evil that we now experience—both material evils like destructive hurricanes and earthquakes and moral evils like war, oppression, murder, abortion, torture, and slavery. There are also questions about who will or has intervened to rescue us from suffering and especially from our alienation from both our Creator and our fellow creatures.

When reading Scripture—just as when reading a mystery story—it's easy for readers to get lost in multiple plot lines and possible answers to the whodunit questions. Through the centuries, as Christians have read through the Old Testament, they have often found themselves distracted by side plots or by apparent solutions that prove to be either illusory or merely partial answers. Even when readers of the Old Testament learn the answer to some of the whodunit questions, such as who created the universe and introduced humans into it, they can become very confused about what kind of creator this is. This is especially true when the question of who is the cause of the universe is combined with the question of who or what is the reason for all the suffering and evil that we experience within this universe. When the questions of creation and evil get intermingled in our experience, it is easy to imagine that either creation is evil or God is somehow an angry God whom we should fear and try to avoid.

As Christians continue to read through Scripture and eventually arrive at the New Testament, however, they find more satisfactory solutions to human anxieties, as well as answers to their questions about who God is and what kind of a creator he is. In the New Testament, Christians discover a set of narratives that summarize the confusingly multiple plot lines of the Old Testament in a kind of recapitulation, summary, or master narrative that sheds light on all the particular narratives of Scripture. In a mystery novel, the final chapter provides a summary from all the plot lines that clearly reveals "whodunit and why and how." Similarly, the New Testament clearly reveals for Christians the "whodunit and why and how" of the mysteries of the Bible.

Reading the Bible as Christians Today

Once Christians know the answers to the whodunit questions, there is diminished value in their rereading the Old Testament from the time-bound perspectives of the original Hebrew readers or hearers. Contrary to many recent trends in scriptural studies and teaching, I am convinced that there is generally more spiritual and theological benefit for Christians from reading the earlier parts of the Bible as the Christian Old Testament than from reading them as "Hebrew Scriptures" (other than for historical or interfaith purposes).

From the time of Jesus and the apostles to the time of the patristic writers or church fathers, continuing into the Middle Ages and up to the Enlightenment, Christians read the Old Testament in light of the New Testament. In other words, they read the Bible as Christians, not as the original Israelite hearers of the stories. Likewise today, I believe that Christians can profit from rereading the Old Testament especially in the light of the answers to its whodunit questions that they now know both from the New Testament and from their own Christian experience and traditions of interpretation. For example, Christians now read the accounts in Genesis aware that the one God who created the universe and humans in the Old Testament is actually a Trinity—Father, Son, and Holy Spirit. The original meaning of the texts remains important as a check against misreading biblical passages or misusing them, as some ancient heretics did, to promote their own religious myths or, as some contemporaries do, to promote their non-biblical ideologies. But Catholics today would benefit more from learning what God has to say to them in their life than from focusing entirely on the meaning of biblical texts for their ancient audiences.

Conclusion

Instead of getting lost in the myriad plots and details of the Old and New Testaments, we can learn from the early church fathers to place particular passages within the context of the overarching biblical story of creation of the world and human beings, of human alienation from God, and of God's subsequent efforts to reconcile humanity. With the fathers, we can appreciate that the climax of God's saving acts was the Father's sending the Son to become incarnate in human flesh and nature as truly both God and man. In other words, the climax of the biblical story from our human point of view is when God incarnate entered our story and made our story God's story.

But before we delve deeper into a theological interpretation of Scripture, we will address concerns alluded to at the beginning of this introduction about the failure of many Catholics to read Scripture regularly, and explain how Vatican II responded to such concerns.

Notes

1. Nevertheless, reading the Bible as God's own story does not assume that God dictated his story word for word to the biblical writers, as the Koran has been said to be dictated to the prophet Mohammed. The approach and corresponding title to this book presume the Catholic teachings that God inspired human authors of Scripture, each of whom wrote using his own respective theology, language, and style. See the *Catechism of the Catholic Church* (Vatican City: Libreria Editrice Vaticana; Washington, DC: United States Catholic Conference, 2000) § 105–8, "Inspiration and Truth of Sacred Scripture," and § 134–41, "In Brief."

2. David C. Steinmetz has a very creative and fruitful comparison of reading the Bible to reading a mystery story, "Uncovering a Second Narrative: Detective Fiction and the Construction of Historical Method," in Ellen F. Davis and Richard B. Hays, eds., *The Art of Reading Scripture* (Grand Rapids, MI: Wm. B. Eerdmans, 2003), pp. 54–65.

3. Gnostic philosophies and religions emphasize that we are saved not by a savior like Jesus who died for us, but simply by knowledge (Greek *gnōsis*) of the truth about who we really are. For example, Gnostics considered themselves as having "inside knowledge" that they are in fact divine sparks trapped in material bodies. Salvation, therefore, comes from knowing this truth so that we can seek to be delivered from our body and its hindrances. It is amazing how such

ancient Gnostic attitudes keep resurfacing, even in the twenty-first century, as in the extremely popular novel by Dan Brown, *The Da Vinci Code: A Novel* (New York: Doubleday, 2003), and in the movie based on it. For a brief readily available description of ancient Gnosticism, see "Gnosticism" in the *Catholic Encyclopedia*, which can be accessed for free at *http://www.newadvent.org/cathen/06592a.htm*.

4. Robert Louis Wilken, "*In Dominico Eloquio*: Learning the Lord's Style of Language," *Communio* 24 (Winter 1997) 846–66, p. 851. Later, Wilken relates to the incarnation the phrase "wonderful things" in Cyril of Alexandria about Isaiah 25:1: "thou hast done wonderful things, a faithful plan formed of old" (Wilken's citation). "In 25:1 he notices the phrase 'a faithful plan formed of old.' This expression and the words 'wonderful things,' says Cyril, refer to the 'mystery of the Incarnation of the only Son and the things that have happened all over the earth because of the Incarnation' [citing Patrologia Graeca 70, 556]."

Wilken also makes a very important distinction relating to historical and theological interpretation of Scripture. "The historical meaning [of an Old Testament passage] is not the full meaning. Once we have seen the divine Son in human flesh, we are able to discern aspects of what happened (or what was said) in the past that were not apparent to earlier generations. Christ's coming not only alters the future, it also reorients the past" (p. 852).

CHAPTER 1

RESPONDING TO THE MANDATES OF VATICAN II

Before Vatican II, Catholics had not usually been encouraged to read the Bible. Personal Bible reading by ordinary Catholics was not a particularly vital part of Catholic tradition. In the mindset of many Catholics, Bible readers were mostly Protestants. Catholics "in the pew" tended to learn about God and about their faith primarily from Catholic catechism classes, religious education, Sunday Mass and sermons, and religious devotions.

The Second Vatican Council made a concerted effort to change such mindsets among Catholic laity. *Dei Verbum* (The Dogmatic Constitution on Divine Revelation) strongly encouraged that Scripture be returned to the center of ordinary Catholic life, worship, liturgy, devotions, and practice. *Dei Verbum* reminded Catholics that the church

> has always maintained [the Scriptures], and continues to do so, together with sacred tradition, as the supreme rule of faith, since, as inspired by God and committed once and for all to writing, they impart the word of God Himself without change, and make the voice of the Holy Spirit resound in the words of the prophets and Apostles.[1]

If the Scriptures "impart the word of God himself" and enable the Holy Spirit's voice to be heard in the written words of the biblical writers, Catholics should desire to make them the center of their faith life and practice. Therefore, *Dei Verbum* goes on to recommend that both religion in general and preaching in particular "be nourished and regulated by Sacred Scripture":

> For in the sacred books, the Father who is in heaven meets His children with great love and speaks with them; and the force and power in the word of God is so great that it stands as the support and energy of the Church, the strength of faith for her sons, the food of the soul, the pure and everlasting source of spiritual life. (§ 21)

One of the most noticeable effects of Vatican II was the addition of more Scripture readings to the Mass, so that by 1970, three Scripture passages were read every Sunday and at least two every weekday, plus responsorial psalms and alleluia verses. The new three-year cycle for Sunday readings and two-year cycle for weekday readings also expanded the range of biblical texts that were covered. In addition, all the sacramental and funeral rituals are based on readings from Scripture. So, at least Catholics who frequently attend Mass, as well as those who frequently participate in the sacraments, already do read or hear a great deal of the Bible.

If God our Father meets us in love and speaks with us in the Bible, then surely we his children will want to listen to what he says to us by reading his word in Scripture. And if the Scriptures are an essential part of Mass and the sacraments, then surely one might expect Catholic pastors to be eager for their parishioners to read Scripture personally. Unfortunately, it is not that simple.

For example, many pastors continue to be afraid that if ordinary Catholics read the Bible without clear supervision, they will be confused and tempted to join various groups of "Bible Christians." For example, as part of my Jesuit training, I spent the summer of 1978 in Nigeria helping a Jesuit missionary by giving weekend biblical institutes to lay Catholics, especially to charismatic prayer groups. One Nigerian pastor spoke for many of his fellow pastors when he said something to this effect: "Catholics should not read the Bible. It confuses them. They should read their catechism instead."

I was reminded of this comment when a pastor in a Latino parish made a very similar statement to me in fall of 2005. I don't remember his exact words, but the gist was this: "I don't want my parishioners to read the Bible, because they get crazy ideas, especially from the Old Testament, such as a God of vengeance." Behind such statements lie genuine pastoral concerns about Catholics misreading Scripture, picking up inappropriate notions about God, and becoming vulnerable to aggressive "Bible Protestants" who would use the Bible to argue ill-informed Catholics away from the Catholic Church into their various denominations or sects (which were very active in Nigeria in the late 1970s, and are so today both in Latin America and among Latino communities in the United States).

Nevertheless, such statements and attitudes by Catholic pastors are truly saddening. Even in response to aggressive proselytizing, the answer is not to keep Catholics away from Scripture. A more adequate pastoral answer would be two-pronged. The first response should be to encourage Catholics to read Scripture. Second and at the same time, we need to help them to read

Scripture as Catholics in order to avoid the literalist and often anti-Catholic interpretations that might lead unsuspecting and ignorant lay Catholics to doubt or leave their faith. Unfortunately, even many of those in pastoral authority who try to protect their lay flocks from anti-Catholic interpretations tend to do so by means of such a heavy dose of historical criticism—which emphasizes almost exclusively the historical original meaning of the text—that the Bible remains an alien book that their people cannot relate meaningfully to their own lives.

Historical criticism seeks the original meaning of a Scripture passage in its ancient historical and cultural context. Unfortunately, explanations of Scripture that are almost exclusively grounded in historical criticism tend to make the meaning of the biblical words and passages sound even more alien and unfamiliar to contemporary daily Catholic living than when they are naively read at their face value. Most ordinary Catholics (and the even greater majority of young people, such as my undergraduate college students) have very little interest in ancient history. If they are going to read Scripture at all, they primarily want to know what it means for them in their lives today.

Knowing what Paul meant in the first century is not always easy to translate into what God may be saying to us today through Paul's words. These original meanings of Paul become less alien and strange, however, if they are further explained in the context of the overall saving message of Scripture as a whole and as expounded and developed in Catholic tradition through homilies and teachings of church fathers and through Catholic creeds, doctrines, and theology. Encouraging ordinary Catholics to read Scripture must also include helping them to read the Bible in light of their overall Catholic faith and practice.

Ignorance of both Scripture and the Catholic faith is not merely a missionary problem, nor is it limited to the poor. Extensive personal experience, both preaching in parishes and also teaching thirty-plus years at a Catholic university, have convinced me of the frightening level of Catholic ignorance of God's word in Scripture and as taught by the Catholic Church. Even university students who can claim twelve years of CCD or Catholic education on the primary and secondary levels share for the most part in this astounding ignorance. As a result, my undergraduate university teaching has become focused primarily on laying a foundation by teaching freshmen the *Catechism of the Catholic Church* with the help of and in the light of Scripture, whereas my upper division courses in New Testament try to enable Catholic and other interested undergraduates to read the Bible intelligently as Catholics and Christians.

Why Should Catholics Read the Bible?

It is essential that Catholics of all ages begin to read the Bible and apply its teachings to their everyday lives. Catholic ignorance of Scripture, especially of Bible stories and of the biblical worldview, can have grave pastoral consequences. If multiple Catholic generations are ignorant of biblical stories and of the Catholic biblical worldview, other worldviews and stories will rush in to fill the vacuum. Some of these will be fundamentalist (and often erroneous) biblical worldviews that lead many Catholics away from their faith. A recent example of such an alien, supposedly biblical, worldview that has confused many Catholics is the hugely successful "Left Behind" series of novels, which promotes a non-biblical view that the pious will be "raptured" to heaven and spared from the "tribulations" of God's judgment descending on unbelievers. Among these "unbelievers," who do not take the Bible literally, Catholics are prominently featured.[2]

Even more widespread and destructive for the future of Catholicism are the secular, materialist, relativist, self-centered, and other unbelieving worldviews on the meaning of life that are forming especially younger generations. Children and youth are imbibing quite alien views on life from their schools, peers, TV, cartoons, movies, the Internet, and other media. Despite sincere efforts by many Catholic parents to pass on their religious and moral views on life, often their children are more influenced by the views they pick up from friends, secular media, clothing fashions, chat rooms, and politically-correct propaganda. Not surprising, then, children at unexpectedly young ages engage in destructive and openly immoral activity, and often take on nihilistic or relativistic attitudes towards life, morality, and worldviews about the meaning of life (or lack thereof).

If Catholic parents do not immerse their children from very young ages in Bible stories and Catholic and biblical views on life, they will be vulnerable to competing worldviews and practices. The stakes can be frightening. No less than our children's eternal salvation could be at risk if we do not manage to convince them of biblical worldviews. We've already witnessed disturbing percentages of young people who, during or after college and even during their high school years, abandon Catholic teachings, practice, and morality. Large numbers of young Catholics are tolerant of almost any religious or secular viewpoint or sexual "lifestyle," unless that viewpoint is "strict" traditional Catholicism. Considerable numbers of young adults are cohabitating without marriage or entering into non-Catholic and civil marriages, and generally living lives with little discernible influence from the Catholic religion into which they were baptized and even confirmed.

Obviously, it is not enough to imbue one's sons and daughters with Catholic and biblical perspectives, teachings, and guidance as young children. This Catholic biblical education has to continue in convincing and persuasive manners through elementary school, middle school, high school, and even the university level. Only then can it counter alien and harmful ideologies, practices, and worldviews to which the young will be exposed in their education and through the heavy use that so many children and youth make of TV, music, computers, the Internet, and video games.

However, these are primarily negative reasons why Catholics should read the Bible, highlighting the conceivable harm of the lack of a biblical worldview. Let us repeat the question, but focus on more positive considerations: How can Catholics benefit from reading the Bible?

Most important, Catholics need to read and know the Bible because the Bible is God's own story and revelation of both himself and the meaning of life. The Bible is the ultimate and primary source and inspiration for Catholic worship, institutions, doctrines, teachings, practices, spiritualities, and worldviews. The Bible is also the common source and guideline that we Catholics share with our brothers and sisters in Orthodox and Protestant denominations. Biblical grounding and the foundations in Catholic faith and morality make sense of what might otherwise be merely arbitrary views of the meaning of life. For example, *why* should we transform social structures?

By reading the Bible, we come to know God, who reveals himself to us in the Scriptures. Moreover, we get to see God's perspective, God's holistic portrayal about the meaning of life. For the writers of the books of the Bible, as well as among the rabbis and Christian church fathers afterward, the most effective way to communicate life's meaning was through the stories of Scripture. Not only children but also adults crave and need meaningful stories to help them to organize life's chaotic experiences into a coherent picture of the meaning of life and of the universe and of the relationship of God to humans.

Ultimately, we believe that the Bible is God's revelation about himself and about the meaning of the universe and of human life (and afterlife) and destiny. But to draw out these meanings from the widely divergent stories and teachings in Scripture, Christians need the guidance of creeds and traditional interpretations of the Bible. Unfortunately, when Catholics seldom read the Bible itself, or if, when they do read Scripture, they do so with no reference to the creeds and tradition, or are taught essentially only the historical meanings of biblical texts, they often fail to experience Scripture as God's revelation to us today. Regrettably, therefore, many concerned young Catholics seeking to learn the Catholic faith have bypassed Scripture altogether and concentrated their study almost exclusively on learning the *Catechism* and doctrinal and moral teachings of the church. Thus, they unconsciously implement the pessimistic views about the value of Scripture for Catholics expressed by the Nigerian and Latino pastors whom I cited earlier.

However, centuries of Catholic teaching, preaching, and incorporating the Bible into Catholic communal and personal lives plus the renewed emphasis on Scripture by Vatican II's *Dei Verbum*, mean that all Catholic life and teaching must be founded on and implement God's biblical revelation. That revelation shows us the true meaning of life and the world. It is God's revelation in Scripture, as interpreted in the tradition of the church and by the magisterium (the church's official teachers) that provides the basis and grounding for all Catholic doctrine and moral teaching. Scripture and its "Bible stories" provide God's fundamental account of the meaning of creation and life. God's underlying story of life's meaning is what the church fathers taught Christians of their day, and what, I think, we should again be teaching the Catholic faithful today.

All Catholics could benefit immensely in their understandings and viewpoints about the meaning of life if they were to read and pray the Bible more frequently and earnestly. But if they are to grow in their Catholic faith and practice from reading Scripture, they need to read the Bible as Catholics, within Catholic traditions and life, learning from the example of Catholic saints, and with the guidance of the creeds, church doctrines, and the contemporary teachings of the pastors and official teachers of the Catholic Church. Otherwise, regular reading of Scripture by Catholics can continue to lead poorly catechized Catholics away from the Catholic Church into more literalist biblical Christian sects. This is the fear that has led to the unfortunate statements and attitudes of Catholic pastors, quoted above, that Catholics should not read the Bible but should read their catechism instead. Regularly reading the Bible with the guidance of the *Catechism* and other Catholic sources, however, can overcome the either-or dichotomy that has plagued and impoverished the spiritual lives of both Catholics and Protestants for centuries. The most complete exposure to and understanding God's word by Catholics can be expected to occur through their reading Scripture with the help of traditional sources.

The Double Mandate of Vatican II to Catholic Biblicists

Vatican II's *Dei Verbum* gave Catholic biblical scholars a double mandate. Its best-known recommendation was that biblicists should study the human aspects of the scriptural text and the meaning that the text had for its original author and audience. The second request of Catholic scholars made by the council fathers was to "read Scripture in the Spirit in which it was written" (*Dei Verbum* § 12; cf. *Catechism of the Catholic Church* § 112–14). The Vatican II document thus commissioned Catholic biblical scholars to learn and teach not only the literal senses of Scripture but also its spiritual meaning as the word of God to believing readers in every place and time. Catholic biblicists have enthusiastically implemented only the first half of this double mandate. Since Vatican II, scholars, religious education teachers, and preachers have extensively investigated and explained the historical and literal meanings of Scripture, but much less so its theological or spiritual meanings as God's word.

One probable reason why this second invitation has been less emphasized is that it presumes that interpreters will read Scripture with the belief that it is God's word addressed to them. It presumes a dynamic belief that the same Holy Spirit who guided the writing of the Bible will also guide believers who read Scripture to understand it as God wants it to be understood. The invitation thus embodies the belief that in reading Scripture, believers will encounter God's revelation and will for themselves. Unfortunately, such emphasis on the interpreter's religious faith in reading and expounding Scripture has often been treated as a source of embarrassment in academic settings, even in many seminaries.

Dei Verbum and its summary in the *Catechism* mention three attitudes toward reading Scripture in the spirit in which it was written: first, to treat Scripture as a *unity* (*Catechism* § 112);[3] second, to read Scripture from within the living *tradition* of the church (§ 113); and third, to interpret Scripture by the *analogy of faith* (§ 114), by the mutual coherence of religious truths in God's saving plan.

Catholics treat Scripture as a *unity,* because by faith they believe that God is the primary author of Scripture. Therefore, they can legitimately expect a unity of purpose, fundamental message, and underlying worldview among the writings of multiple human biblical authors whom the one and same God has inspired and guided. Believers expect this unity of purpose and worldview even when the biblical authors' individual perspectives and theologies differ among themselves in details, sometimes even dramatically.[4] For example, believers would be surprised to encounter in Scripture two human authors, one who unambiguously portrays Jesus as divine, whereas another explicitly maintains the opposite argument that Jesus is merely human. Both Jews and Christians believe that in Scripture God does not directly contradict himself.

Believing Catholics, therefore, approach the various human authors and texts of Scripture with a *hermeneutics of faith*, interpreting it with empathy, understanding, and consent.[5] They generally refrain from a *hermeneutics of suspicion*, which actively searches for biblical contradictions as openings that might legitimize readers' opinions that are incompatible with those spelled out in the Scripture.[6] They focus more on biblical intertextuality, the study of mutual interrelationships of words, themes, and passages within the books of Scripture, and on the interplay and interpretive assistance of related biblical evidence, rather than on lining up differences and apparent contradictions.[7]

Catholic interpreters find and contextualize this biblical unity not only within the limits of the canon or official collection of biblical books, but also within the living *tradition* of the church. They experience church tradition in liturgy and sacraments, in church doctrines and teachings, in the writings of ancient, medieval, and modern Catholic thinkers and teachers, and in Catholic spiritual and moral theology, up to and including the present-day guidance of Catholics by the magisterium (official church teaching authorities) in union with the pope.

Hence, as a Catholic interpreter, I customarily search the Bible with guidance from my pre-existing Catholic belief system. I do not approach Scripture with a "purely objective" mind that is a *tabula rasa*, "blank slate," but with one that has been formed by many years of learning and experience as a Catholic. This implies that when I consult Scripture, I usually anticipate that the biblical answer will not be completely alien to what I already know and hold as a Catholic. Nevertheless, anyone for whom Scripture is God's word has to be ready for the possibility that God's word might jar believers by a radically new awareness into modifying their opinion about what they had previously considered to be God's revelation. However, even then, the dialogue between this new insight from God's biblical word and what they had previously embraced as the truth will start from their previous Catholic convictions.

All this, in turn, is very closely related to interpreting what we find in Scripture by the *analogy of faith* (*Catechism* § 114), that is, by the coherence of truths of faith among themselves within God's saving plan.[8] In fact this coherence of truths is plainly related to a Catholic biblical worldview. Whatever biblical texts I read that might shed light on Jesus, I spontaneously contextualize by my own personal and pastoral experience of believing in Jesus. This includes my worship of Jesus in personal prayer and at the Eucharist, my preaching and teaching about Jesus as both God and man, and the like. The analogy of faith facilitates a harmony in one's faith between what one reads in Scripture and one's related experience.

Turning Points in Catholic Biblical Interpretation

As indicated earlier in this chapter, a momentous turning point for recent Catholic approaches to Scripture was the publication of *Dei Verbum* by the Second Vatican Council on November 18, 1965. During the nineteenth and twentieth centuries, Catholic teaching authorities (the magisterium) had been inclined to resist elements of modernism and the Enlightenment in biblical studies, because they were undermining belief in miracles and doctrines, and in other aspects of Catholic faith.[9] Therefore, authorities had been suspicious of some of the unquestionably modernistic presuppositions and aspects of historical criticism, the academic study of the original meaning of passages in their historical contexts, as applied to Scripture. Some pioneers among Catholic biblical scholars who had begun to incorporate historical criticism into their research and writing suffered because of this suspicion, for example, by being forbidden to publish or teach. Even a half-century later, some of their students and successors continue to mention sufferings that officials in the Vatican had caused for biblical pioneers like Marie-Joseph LaGrange.[10]

After decades of official restriction of Catholic application of historical critical investigation to Scripture, at the end of 1965 Vatican II's *Dei Verbum* definitively endorsed Catholic use of historical criticism for explaining and interpreting Scripture. This dogmatic constitution removed most remaining Vatican hesitations and solidified and greatly accelerated the Catholic Church's embrace of historical critical approaches to the Bible. It reaffirmed Pius XII's encyclical *Divino Afflante Spiritu* (On Promoting Biblical Studies), which had been published about twenty-two years earlier (September 30, 1943), when Catholic magisterial suspicion of and resistance to these critical methods had begun to give way to their acceptance. The way for its reception had been further and more immediately prepared by the Pontifical Biblical Commission's *Sancta Mater Ecclesia* (Instruction on the Historical Truth of the Gospels), dated April 21, 1964.[11]

Once restrictions from church authorities were lifted, Catholic biblical specialists plunged with great enthusiasm and considerable success into historical critical interpretation of Scripture. With surprising rapidity, however, only ten to twenty years after the 1965 publication of *Dei Verbum*, growing grassroots and scholarly dissatisfaction with the limits and negative "side effects" of historical criticism had already caused growing numbers of biblical scholars to begin seriously searching for alternative or at least supplementary approaches to interpreting Scripture. This dissatisfaction came from even opposite ends of the spectrum of theological opinion.

Pentecostal Christians and charismatic Catholics and Protestants, especially, objected to the historical reductionism and skepticism of historical criticism, which tended to deny the reality of miracles and of God's intervention into believers' lives. Liberation and feminist interpreters became frustrated that historical criticism relegated most significant meaning of Scripture into a past that is long dead and gone, with little to offer those suffering from oppression today. From the mid to late 1980s, literary and narrative critical and reader-response approaches to Scripture were rapidly imported from secular literary criticism into biblical studies as partial correctives.[12]

Hopes of ordinary readers for an approach to teaching and reading Scripture more amenable to their Catholic faith were soon disappointed, however. Increasingly radical developments in biblical interpretation and rejections of historical criticism gained momentum as postmodernism more and more fully supplanted modernist approaches to history and literary criticism. A pivotal modernist assumption of historical criticism, the possibility of an objective reading of Scripture free from readers' presuppositions, became convincingly refuted by postmodern demonstrations that all readers bring their previous experiences, understanding, and questions to the understanding of any text, including Scripture. In turn, the interpretive biases of postmodern scholars in their reconstructed scriptural histories or revisionist biblical interpretations, which "rewrote" biblical history or radically reinterpreted biblical teachings, became increasingly obvious. These problematic tendencies appeared in many forms, whether the particular scholars were promoting changes in a particular religious denomination, through a liberationist or materialist ideology, or in unbelieving forms of secularism, agnosticism, or atheism.

Some extreme forms of these developments appeared under the rubric of "deconstruction." Whereas many idealistic philosophies from the modernist enlightenment period had denied that our human intellect and reason can know realities external to our mental perceptions, images, or concepts of them, deconstructive philosophies went even further. Some forms of deconstruction denied that human minds can know even mental ideas or concepts.[13]

According to more extreme deconstructive perspectives, therefore, words do not even refer to concepts in our minds. Rather, words are used solely as instruments of power to advance the speaker or writer's agenda and ideology. If words no longer have intrinsic meaning nor refer to external or even internal reality on any level, they can be used to mean whatever the speaker or writer wants them to mean. This stance destroys meaningful human communication and replaces it with partisan ideological and political power struggles. Believing readers of Scripture can find little comfort in such extreme conclusions.

In the last forty years, therefore, many Catholic biblical scholars have found themselves riding an emotional rollercoaster between energizing scholarly achievements and discouragingly harmful side effects, for which the opportunities were opened by Vatican II's endorsement of historical critical methods. In addition to a natural sense of relief and new freedom, Catholic biblicists initially enjoyed several decades of exhilarating new advances by using these approaches and became fully accepted into the guild of biblical scholars of all denominations and of academe.

Before very long, however, this excitement became vulnerable to fresh concerns and frustrations among both scholars and ordinary Catholics interested in Scripture, concerning the limitations and negative consequences of the new approaches. As believing scholars realized that the modernistic period that followed the Enlightenment was giving way to postmodernism in the 1980s, they were likely to experience both relief and new misgivings. The transition brought some relief from their frustrations with the narrow limits of historical critical approaches. Yet, it also brought a growing awareness of how radical and hostile to traditional religion some of these newer ways of interpreting Scripture were becoming.

The recent shift by many Catholic, other Christian, and Jewish biblical specialists toward explicitly and unapologetically *theological* interpretation of Scripture, as well as their revival of models and interpretive writings of premodern biblical interpreters, are raising new hopes among both scholars and ordinary readers of Scripture that Catholic biblical scholarship is finally moving earnestly toward a more balanced response to both of the mandates of Vatican II. As some forms of interpretation are becoming ever more hostile to Catholic (and other religious) beliefs and ever more rebellious against any forms of church authority or any limits on one's interpretive or moral autonomy, growing numbers of Catholic, Protestant, and Jewish scholars are trying to retrieve what is useful and helpful from our premodern forerunners to assist us in relating as believers to our postmodern future.

Broadening the "Intention of the Author" and the "Literal Sense" of Scripture

One important insight that is facilitating this intensifying turn to theological interpretation is the broadening of the notion of the *literal sense* of Scripture beyond the intention of the human author. Even more significant is the move beyond equating the human intention with the results of historical criticism (some think this may be implied even in the Pontifical Biblical Commission's *The Interpretation of the Bible in the Church*).[14] David Williams effectively challenges the widespread practice among interpreters and even some church documents of limiting the literal sense of Scripture to the meaning intended and written by the human author. In *Receiving the Bible in Faith: Historical and Theological Exegesis,* Williams provides arguments for reconsidering and broadening the biblical author's intention to include not only that of the human author but also the intention of the divine author.[15]

Contemporary Catholic biblicists do not have to create *ex nihilo*, "from nothing," their investigations into the intentions of God as primary author of Scripture. In Catholic tradition, as I mentioned earlier, patristic writers (ancient church fathers) had already exemplified ways to broaden the notion of "meaning intended by the author" that is utilized in *Dei Verbum* to include not only the human author and his historical audience but also God as the divine author *of all Scripture*. If the search for the intention of the biblical author is limited to the various human authors and their historically discoverable intentions, historical criticism inevitably becomes privileged as the almost exclusive instrument for ascertaining those intentions.

The divine author's intention, however, is clearly beyond the scope of historical methods. The discovery of God's intention requires faith and explicitly theological interpretation, in addition to historical investigation. The meaning and contexts that point to the divine author's intent necessitate that scholars consult also the canonical level of the final Old and New Testament biblical collection, as well as Catholic tradition (especially the church's traditions of biblical interpretation) and the contemporary Catholic magisterium.

Once one acknowledges the divine author of all of Scripture and of each of its individual books, faith and theological thinking have to supplement more conventional historical, linguistic, and grammatical approaches toward understanding the words and meanings of the biblical text. Acknowledgment of God as the Bible's primary author moves Catholic and other religiously motivated biblical scholars beyond the criteria and interpretive practices of their fellow biblical practitioners in academic guilds, meetings, and educational institutions, even in seminaries and schools of theology. Academic interpretation and exegesis tends to focus almost exclusively on individual human biblical authors and writings, or often even on stages within biblical writings.

That focus considers almost exclusively the diversity within the many books of Scripture and is unable to articulate what unity there might be among the numerous authors and writings in the Bible. Historical criticism routinely and *a priori* excludes consideration of God as biblical author. Doing so also prevents recognition of Scripture as God's word and revelation. If Scripture is not regarded as the word and revelation of God, its primary author, ascertaining the Bible's unity becomes almost impossible. Meaningful unity of Scripture can be recognized only if one believes that the Bible has one ultimate divine author revealing his word and message of salvation. Without reflection on the one divine author, it is hard to demonstrate any significant sense of biblical unity.

Increasing numbers of Catholic interpreters have come to

realize that it is not possible to continue putting off indefinitely a more substantial response to Vatican II's insistence on the church's doctrine that Scripture is God's word and revelation, even though *Dei Verbum* had also accentuated previously under-appreciated human dimensions of the biblical writings. Catholic scholars have begun moving beyond their initial excitement over the relative novelty of Catholic dedication to academic forms of historical critical interpretation. They have become more aware of its shortcomings and limitations for faith, for the life of the church, and for the needs of contemporary believers. Ordinary Catholic readers should be encouraged by this development.

Conclusion

As Catholic scholars have progressively refocused on the divine aspects of Scripture as God's word, they have found themselves increasingly attracted to the example and writings of the patristic and medieval authors who focused primarily on these divine attributes of Scripture. Because of their relatively more intense appreciation of the humanity of the Bible and its authors, contemporary Catholic scholars are not tempted to return to theological flights of fancy of some premodern authors. They are, nevertheless, seeking insights from premodern interpretation for understanding the theological meaning of Scripture in ways that seem legitimate to contemporary mindsets without getting distracted by some of premodern interpreters' obsolete and no longer viable ways of reading the Bible. The following chapters will turn to early church fathers for examples of how to read Scripture theologically today.[16]

Notes

1. *Dei Verbum* (Dogmatic Constitution on Divine Revelation), § 21, accessed September 2006 from the Vatican Web site at *http://www.vatican.va/ archive/hist_councils/ii_vatican_council/documents/vat-ii_const_19651118 _dei-verbum_en.html*.

2. Tim F. LaHaye and Jerry B. Jenkins, *Left Behind: A Novel of the Earth's Last Days* (Wheaton, IL: Tyndale House Publishers, 1995) is the first of many books in the series.

3. Treating Scripture as a unity partially overlaps (in practice, though less in theory) some contemporary scholarly emphases on biblical intertextuality or intratextuality. My own use of intertextuality (i.e., study of mutual interrelationships of words, themes, and passages within the books of Scripture) differs from pure literary influence in that it does not focus principally on causality or priority (such as the influence of Old Testament texts on New Testament texts). It also treats the present relationship of both Old and New Testament texts within the biblical canon: contemporary readers can mutually interpret both texts by each other, regardless of chronological priority. This seems to me to be also inherent in the patristic and traditional notion of the unity of Scripture. Paul Dinter approvingly cites "an ancient hermeneutical insight: the Bible can be read as a self-glossing book" (Paul A. Dinter, "The Once and Future Text," *The Quest for Context and Meaning: Studies in Biblical Intertextuality in Honor of James A. Sanders*, ed. Craig A. Evans and Shemaryahu Talmon [Biblical Interpretation Series, 28; Leiden: Brill, 1997], 375–92, p. 385 quoting G. L. Bruns, "Midrash and Allegory . . ." in Robert Alter and Frank Kermode, eds., *The Literary Guide to the Bible* [Cambridge: Belknap, 1987], p. 26).

4. See Peter S. Williamson, *Catholic Principles for Interpreting Scripture: A Study of the Pontifical Biblical Commission's* The Interpretation of the Bible in the Church (Rome: Editrice Pontificio Istituto Biblico, 2001), pp. 117–27.

5. Williamson treats these topics under the rubric of a "hermeneutic of faith" (*Catholic Principles*, pp. 95–108). Cf. Joseph Ratzinger, "Biblical Interpretation in Crisis: On the Question of the Foundations and Approaches of Exegesis Today," in *Biblical Interpretation in Crisis: The Ratzinger Conference on Bible and Church*, ed. Richard John Neuhaus (Grand Rapids: Eerdmans and the Rockford Institute Center on Religion and Society, 1989), pp. 1–23, esp. pp. 22–23.

6. Cf. Williamson, *Catholic Principles*, pp. 231–32; William S. Kurz, *Read-*

ing Luke-Acts: Dynamics of Biblical Narrative (Louisville, KY: Westminster/ John Knox Press, 1993), pp. 173–76.

7. Cf. Williamson, *Catholic Principles*, pp. 72, 118–21, 191, *passim* ("repeatedly").

8. Cf. Williamson, *Catholic Principles*, pp. 100–8.

9. Modernism involves many intellectual and cultural movements that sharply emphasized "modern" thought and movements over against ancient, medieval, and traditional thinking. In church history, modernism peaked at the turn from the nineteenth to twentieth centuries and was especially critical of church "superstition" and "corrupt" authorities and practices. In biblical studies, it featured rationalism, i.e., a glorification of reasoning from experimental evidence over faith. It included historicism, a reduction of truth to only what can be historically proven. The various forms of modernism have their ultimate roots in the eighteenth-century Enlightenment, which produced philosophical movements emphasizing the use of reason to challenge doctrines and traditions in many fields of knowledge, including religion. Recently, strong movements under the label "postmodernism" have arisen in literary and other forms of criticism and thought, which are challenging and overturning the presuppositions of modernism.

10. For a very brief account of Marie-Joseph Lagrange, OP (1855–1938), who founded the prestigious École Biblique ("school of biblical studies") in Jerusalem in 1890, the scholarly biblical journal the *Revue Biblique* in 1892, and a series of scholarly commentaries on the Bible, the *Études Bibliques,* in 1903, see "Lagrange, Marie-Joseph," in *Encyclopædia Britannica.* Retrieved June 7, 2006, from Encyclopædia Britannica Premium Service: http:// www.britannica.com/eb/article-9046838. Though loyal to church authority, Lagrange's commentary on Genesis (1906) was interpreted as sharing the modernist viewpoint that the church was then resisting. Lagrange was strongly criticized, until "in 1912 opposition to some of his methods caused his superiors to recall him to France. He was later sent back to Jerusalem, where he taught, except during World War I, until his death."

11. For these and other related magisterial texts, see the very useful collection, *The Scripture Documents: An Anthology of Official Catholic Teachings,* ed. & trans. Dean P. Bechard; foreword by Joseph A. Fitzmyer (Collegeville, MN: Liturgical Press, 2002).

12. Cf. William S. Kurz, *Reading Luke-Acts.*

13. For criticisms of deconstruction, see M. H. Abrams, "Construing and

Deconstructing," in *Deconstruction: A Critique*, ed. Rajnath (London: The Macmillan Press Ltd., 1989), pp. 68–92; J. H. Hunter, "Deconstruction and Biblical Texts: Introduction and Critique," *Neotestamentica* 21 (1987) pp. 125–40; and Kurz, *Reading Luke-Acts*, 172–83, notes pp. 217–19.

14. Pontifical Biblical Commission, *The Interpretation of the Bible in the Church* (Boston: St. Paul Books & Media, 1993), 82–87, esp. "The Literal Sense," pp. 82–84. See especially the critiques and discussion of this document in Peter S. Williamson, *Catholic Principles for Interpreting Scripture: A Study of the Pontifical Biblical Commission's* The Interpretation of the Bible in the Church (Subsidia Biblica; Rome: Editrice Pontificio Istituto Biblico, 2001), pp. 163–70, 181–88.

15. David M. Williams, *Receiving the Bible in Faith: Historical and Theological Exegesis* (Washington, DC: The Catholic University of America Press, 2004), pp. 179–98.

16. See Appendix, "A Conversation about the Future of Catholic Biblical Scholarship," for some recent developments among scholars who are trying to find more theological approaches to the biblical text.

CHAPTER 2

DEVELOPING A THEOLOGICAL APPROACH TO SCRIPTURE

Scripture scholars interested in finding a more explicitly theological and less exclusively historical approach toward interpreting Scripture don't have to start from scratch. Catholics have centuries' worth of examples of theological readings of Scripture to draw upon—beginning in the Bible itself in the later Old Testament and the New Testament, flourishing through the patristic and medieval periods, up until the widespread rejection of those "precritical" interpretative approaches in the modernist age. A significant, if partial, reason for that rejection was Enlightenment rationalism and its rejection of dogma.[1]

Catholics today can learn much from the church fathers about how to read Scripture theologically as God's word. Although the fathers are popularly known especially for their use of "four spiritual senses" and for their varying emphases on allegory, these are not the approaches followed in this book. More helpful for our purposes is the way Sts. Irenaeus and Athanasius, in particular, read all of Scripture and each individual passage within the perspective of God's overarching biblical story of creation and salvation as the key to the meaning of the entire canonical Bible, from Genesis to Revelation. This biblical story is summarized in the church's "rule of faith," which the church fathers also consult in interpreting biblical passages.

Allegory and the Other "Senses" of Scripture

Controversies exist among Catholic and other Christian biblical and historical scholars over ancient and medieval interpretive approaches, such as the multiple "senses," or kinds of interpretations, of Scripture, and especially the fathers' much-criticized use of allegory. And not only patristic and medieval but some contemporary biblical specialists continue to have high regard for allegorical interpretation of biblical passages. Rather than join such disputes, I will try to highlight other aspects of patristic interpretation that might be more readily and widely acceptable today. Actually, reading Scripture theologically with help from the patristic writers does not necessarily require understanding, mastering, or using the "four senses" of patristic and medieval interpretation. Nor do contemporary biblical scholars necessarily need to learn or make extensive use of ancient allegorical approaches toward Scripture, which some current interpreters find distasteful. Yet, since Sts. Irenaeus and Athanasius provide helpful examples of ways to interpret Scripture, in part because they avoid the use of allegory, it does seem important to explain briefly what is usually meant by allegorical interpretation of Scripture.

The *Catechism of the Catholic Church* provides a readily available summary of the chief distinctions among kinds of interpretation or "senses" of Scripture. Its two major categories are the literal sense and the spiritual senses (*Catechism* § 115–19); the spiritual senses are usually subdivided into the "allegorical, moral, and anagogical senses" (§ 117). The *Catechism* explains that because of the unity of God's saving plan (§ 112), the realities and events about which Scripture speaks can be signs of other realities (§ 117). The three spiritual senses are, therefore, the *allegorical* sense (in which one referent can stand for another, such as crossing the Red See as a sign of Christ's victory and Christian baptism); the *moral* sense (which relates Scripture to acting justly, as "written for our instruction," 1 Corinthians 10:11); and the *anagogical* sense (which relates Scripture to its eternal significance and our future hope, e.g., seeing the church on earth as a sign of the heavenly Jerusalem, *Catechism* § 117).

To "allegorize" a biblical (or any) text usually involves isolating individual words, phrases, or details in the passage from their natural meaning in their original contexts, and then correlating those words with some other word or reality that was not part of the passage's original meaning or context. For example, it was common for Christians in ancient and medieval times to allegorize the two human lovers in the ancient biblical Hebrew love song, the Song of Solomon (or Canticle of Canticles), as referring to the love of Christ for the church, his bride. This example of allegorizing the Song of Solomon suggests that some biblical allegory remains valuable. Christians today still esteem the symbolism of Christ and his bride, the church, which has been especially immortalized in the comparison of husband and wife to Christ and his bridal church in Ephesians 5:21-33. Other examples of patristic or medieval allegorizing—especially those in which the allegorical details are far removed from the central point of the biblical passage—are less attractive today. For instance, there may not be much current interest in allegorizing Martha and Mary, respectively, as active and contemplative spiritualities (for example, of "active" Jesuits and "contemplative" Trappists or Poor Clare sisters).

At the heart of the disputes over approaches like allegory is the extent to which allegory does or does not express or presume the apparently intended meaning of the original human biblical writer. Roland Teske exemplifies the issues at stake in an illuminating case study of Augustine's literal and christological (spiritual) interpretations of the Good Samaritan.[2] Augustine usually interprets this parable christologically (allegorically correlating the Good Samaritan who helps the fallen man with the incarnate Son, who helps fallen humankind). He also, however, can interpret the parable literally (in ways acceptable to historical critics), and he has produced several examples of its literal interpretation. Nevertheless, there is an added theological richness in Augustine's christological interpretation, which can exemplify the entire plan of God's salvation of fallen humanity through the incarnation of the Son. Augustine himself admits the difference between the meaning intended by the human author and a meaning that the text can call to the reader's mind even if it was not part of the author's original point. If the latter spiritual meaning is consistent with the overall message of Scripture as interpreted in the church, Augustine would consider it as a legitimate understanding of the text's message from God to the reader.

Origen was a famous early example of a considerable number of patristic writers who applied allegory when seeking theological meaning from a passage that they found either meaningless or problematic in some way. It was hard, however, to avoid arbitrariness in allegorizing. Allegory often imported meaning from other parts of Scripture or from examples relevant to a later audience's lives into individual words or phrases that were taken out of context. It also frequently applied those words to something unrelated to the original meaning of the passage.

Another important consideration about allegory is that some

New Testament passages had already allegorized Old Testament details. St. Paul himself was used by the church fathers as an early example for allegorizing Old Testament passages and for biblical warrant to import different meanings in place of the original ones. An example is 1 Corinthians 10:1-4, especially verse 4, "And all [the Israelites in the desert] drank from the same supernatural [or *spiritual*] drink. For they drank from the supernatural [*spiritual*] Rock which followed them, *and the Rock was Christ*" (emphasis added).

Another Pauline New Testament example to which patristic writers referred was his allegory in Galatians reversing the original descendants of Abraham's two sons, Ishmael the son of Hagar, the slave woman, who was born "according to the *flesh*," and Isaac the son of the free woman, Sarah, who was born "through *promise*":

Now this is an allegory: these women are two covenants. One is from Mount Sinai, bearing children for slavery; she is Hagar. *Now Hagar is Mount Sinai in Arabia; she corresponds to the present Jerusalem, for she is in slavery with her children. But the Jerusalem above is free, and she is our mother.* (Galatians 4:24-26, emphasis added)

Paul's allegory made sense to his first-century audience, but raises more questions for twenty-first-century readers. It identifies the two women as two covenants, equating "the present Jerusalem" (which was still standing when he wrote Galatians) to an Arabian mountain and claiming that Jerusalem "is in slavery with her children." The mother of Christians is rather "the Jerusalem above" (a striking parallel to the heavenly Jerusalem in Revelation 3:12: "the new Jerusalem which comes down from my God out of heaven"). The heavenly Jerusalem, which is mother of Christians, is free, as are her Christian children.[3]

In their quest for theological meaning, the early Fathers of the Church were less inclined to resort to allegorizing the New Testament than the Old Testament. Nevertheless, some fathers did allegorize New Testament parables and New Testament passages that did not have immediate homiletic or theological application for their readers or audience. One reason for choosing Sts. Irenaeus and Athanasius as our models is that they provide patterns of how to find theological meaning without allegorizing, which usually changes the passage's original meaning. Instead, they relate the passage in its standard meaning to the context of the overall biblical narrative of God's salvation. This approach seems equally promising for theologically interpreting both the Old and New Testaments.

Theological Interpretation by Iraneaus and Athanasius

Approaches of the church fathers that seem more inviting today for interpreting Scripture theologically (as God's biblical message) are exemplified in the writings of Sts. Irenaeus (ca. A.D. 125–203) and Athanasius (A.D. 298–373). Both of these church fathers had to deal with alien or harmful interpretations and applications of Scripture by Gnostic and Arians, which supported non-Christian religious mythology or heretical forms of Christianity that denied central Christian dogmas. The problematical forms of interpretation in both Gnosticism and Arianism tended not only to take words, phrases, or passages out of their natural biblical context. They tended also to read those words or passages with an exaggerated literalist interpretation that failed to respect the overall biblical revelation about the relationship of God to the world and about the history of God's salvation of errant humans. To counter these misleading approaches to Scripture, both Irenaeus and Athanasius explicitly read and interpreted Scripture in the context of the entire biblical message of creation and salvation and of traditional church summaries of biblical revelation in various versions of the "rule of faith."

The genius of early fathers like Irenaeus and Athanasius was to combine two important operations of the biblical exegete and interpreter. The first was a relatively simple and straightforward procedure. Both fathers read each biblical passage quite closely and with intense attention to details in the text, as biblical scholars do today. However, unlike most contemporary academic biblicists, Irenaeus and Athanasius also intentionally read each individual passage in the light of Scripture's essential story line.

Early Christian fathers regularly read and steeped themselves in Scripture and participated in liturgies that featured biblical readings over the course of the church's liturgical year (readings that commemorated most of God's story of salvation). They expressed their personal and communal prayers in the words of the Old Testament psalms, and they consciously lived within the biblical worldview. In these ways, they derived from the Bible an overarching narrative.[4] From the Bible's myriad details, plotlines, books, theologies, and cultural contexts, patristic writers excerpted an underlying unified story line, a foundational biblical story. Commencing from the very beginning—the creation of the world and of humans by God—this story recounted the human fall from God's friendship as well as God's response through divine promises, covenants, saving acts, and the use of human instruments to implement divine providence.

This biblical story finds its climax in the incarnation of the Son of God and in the life, death, and resurrection of Jesus. It continues with the life of the church up until the final judgment. Using this fundamental story as the implied context and background for all the individual accounts and perspectives in both Old and New Testaments enabled the patristic authors to pay extremely close attention to individual details of particular biblical passages without losing a sense of God's overall biblical message.

As a further check against getting lost in the maze of diverging and sometimes apparently even misleading strands among the many Old and New Testament books and authors, the fathers used a "rule of faith," which recapitulated the basic story line of Scripture. They assumed that the Bible's foundational narrative had been authentically summarized by the church in theological and philosophical terminology as the church's rule of faith. This rule of faith was based on scriptural narratives, teachings, and evidence.[5] In turn, this rule of faith also helped to keep readers' bearings focused on the essentials of the overall biblical story and message and not to get lost in voluminous biblical details, stories, and theologies.

Interpreting passages in light of the salvation narrative of Scripture was only one way in which Irenaeus' and Athanasius' approach was ingenious. Their second resourceful step was to express in more systematically theological terminology the essence of the biblical economy or saving narrative. These early fathers found themselves forced to go beyond merely repeating the biblical terms and language to try to express the realities to which they referred or their grounding in the being of God and creation. That was because biblical statements and passages were being quoted out of context in a "proof-texting" manner to endorse false teaching, and biblical terms were being misused to promote misleading human mythologies and doctrinal systems, such as Gnosticism and, later, Arianism, which undermined the Christian faith.

The Rule of Faith and Gnosticism

Gnostics (from the Greek for "knowing") were heretical thinkers who were quite influential at the time of Irenaeus. They claimed to have extra-biblical oral revelation and inside knowledge that ordinary (and implicitly inferior) Catholic Christians did not have. At the heart of their religion was an alien mythology that claimed that human souls were sparks of the divine that somehow got trapped in evil matter. Salvation came primarily through souls' *knowing* their true identity as sparks of the divine and, consequently, being freed from the shackles of their material bodies. Though the ancient Gnostic religion is no longer practiced, Gnostic tendencies occasionally reappear, as in some aspects of recent "New Age" religiosity.

Irenaeus noted that Gnostics took biblical details completely out of their biblical context and significance, and then fashioned their eccentric non-biblical doctrines by using biblical vocabulary in non-biblical ways that even reversed their original sense and meaning. Irenaeus likened their interpretations to taking apart a beautiful mosaic image of a king into its constituent pieces, and then rearranging those pieces into a new mosaic image of a dog.[6] To counter such chaotic and arbitrary proof-texting of biblical words and passages, church leaders emphasized that the Scriptures needed to be read in light of their basic message, which had been summed up in the church's "rule of faith."

For example, when ancient Gnostics took biblical words and passages out of context to elaborate their peculiar polytheistic myths of creation and salvation, which were quite foreign to biblical revelation, Irenaeus insisted on reading biblical words and passages in both their immediate biblical context, and in the context of the church's understanding of the central biblical message.

Since Gnostics put so much emphasis on salvation as achieved by knowledge, they reversed the usual understanding of Genesis 3. They considered the creator god who forbad humans to eat of the tree of knowledge to be an inferior, jealous god who was trying to protect his divine prerogative of knowing good and evil by preventing humans from sharing in such knowledge. The hero of the Gnostic interpretation of Genesis 3 was the serpent, who challenged the jealous prohibition by the creator, because the serpent encouraged the knowledge that humans needed (as sparks of the divine) to be freed from the shackles and limitations of their material bodies. Gnostic interpretations of biblical creation and the world tended to imply a dualism between fundamental principles of Good (spiritual reality) and Evil (material reality), a dualism that eventually would flourish in the form of Manichaeism at the time of St. Augustine.

Gnostics also used a phrase from 2 Corinthians 4:4, "the god of this world," to argue that there is a second god who created and rules our material world, and who is different from God, the Father of Jesus. Their second god (the creator) was jealous, vengeful, and inferior to the New Testament God of love and Father of Jesus Christ. Such arguments implied that the

Gnostics also rejected the Old Testament as Christian revelation. Consequently, Gnostics also implicitly rejected the unity of Scripture, which clearly emphasizes that there is only one God.[7] Never losing sight of the foundational truth, which the Old Testament and Judaism repeatedly emphasize, that there is only one God, the church fathers consistently affirmed the Christian understanding that the God who acts in the Old Testament is the same God who is Father of Jesus in the New Testament. Scholars today generally understand that "the god of this world" in Paul refers to a fairly common belief in the later Old Testament and in the New Testament that Satan had usurped much of Adam's dominion over earth that had been debilitated when Adam rebelled against God. As a Jewish monotheist, Paul certainly was not referring to a second god in the strict sense.

Contrary to Gnosticism and other ancient heretical misinterpretations of Scripture, Irenaeus and other church fathers used the whole story of salvation and the rule of faith to demonstrate that the God who creates, saves his people from Egypt, gives them the Law, promises them a Messiah and Savior from David's line, and sends the prophets to them is actually the Trinity. That is, not only is he the one and only God to whom Judaism has given constant witness, but also this one God is now recognized by Christians to be trinitarian—Father, Son, and Holy Spirit.

The Rule of Faith and Arianism

Rules of faith, such as those used by St. Iranaeus, were tools for theologians and biblical interpreters, whereas creeds were primarily used as professions of faith in the Sacrament of Baptism.[8] Later interpreters and readers of Scripture came to also use official creeds as they would a rule of faith. The most significant creed for biblical interpretation came to be the Nicene Creed, which St. Athanasius helped to formulate at the Council of Nicea in A.D. 325.

The Nicene Creed was defined to counteract the heretical denial of Jesus' divinity by the Arians. Even though the Arians accepted the biblical claim that the Son existed with God before the creation of the material world, they based their denial of his divinity on their interpretation of several biblical passages that seemed to imply that the Son of God was a creature. Compare John 1:1-3, "In the beginning was the Word, and the Word was with God, and the Word was God," with the claim by Wisdom in Proverbs 8:22-23, "The LORD *created me at the beginning of his work*, the first of his acts of old. Ages ago I was set up, at the first, before the beginning of the earth" (emphasis added). In the chapter on Athanasius, we shall see how the principal rejoinders that Athanasius makes against Arian biblical interpretation were for the most part alternative interpretations of the same passages that were being used by Arians to deny Jesus' divinity. As we shall see, he was guided in his close reading by the overall biblical message of salvation as interpreted by the church, in which the divine Son of God was begotten by the Father as equally divine without being a second God.

The church fathers frequently argued that when humans rejected God and his commands in their desire to be like God themselves, no mere human could make up for that offense against God's infinite dignity. Therefore, they often emphasized that the turning point in God's biblical story of salvation was the occasion on which the Second Person of the Trinity (the Son or Word) became man (in the incarnation) to reconcile humans to

God and to "re-open the gates of heaven" as unique mediator between God and man.[9] To be able to function as mediator, God's incarnate Son, Jesus, could not be merely a creature. It is because the Son of God is both truly God and truly man that he can mediate between and reconcile God and the alienated human race. Because the Son is of the same being as the Father, the Son also is God. Thus, the incarnate Jesus is both God and man.[10]

Because of the predominant role played by the incarnation in the biblical account of salvation, the key to Scripture was generally recognized to be the doctrine that the Son was of the same being, nature, or essence as the Father, even though the wording of that teaching is more philosophical than biblical. To expound this doctrine, Athanasius and other church fathers used the philosophical term, *homoousios* (of the same being or essence), which they admitted was not even found in the Bible. They neither found this term or doctrinal teaching explicitly expressed in Scripture, nor did they extract this term from the Bible. Nevertheless, they judged that this word most fully and accurately expressed the fundamental biblical teaching about the Son, that he was not only "with God" in the beginning, before the creation of the world, as the Arians also held, but that he "was God," as John 1:1 put it.[11]

Modern Misinterpretations of Scripture

Almost two millennia ago, the early church teachers discovered the inadequacy of using only the language and terms found in the Bible for orthodox biblical teaching, since false teachers like the Gnostics and the Arians were taking biblical terms utterly out of their biblical contexts. To counter these heresies, the church fathers needed to use the rule of faith and find wording that, even if it were non-biblical, could faithfully convey the meaning of Scripture texts. It seems ironic, then, that today certain fundamentalist biblicists are again insisting on finding all Christian teachings in Scripture alone, and also in *using only biblical language* to express contemporary Christian beliefs.

Literalist biblicism that refuses to entertain any theological expressions that are not found verbatim in Scripture is powerless to counter misquotation and misuse of biblical expressions and passages for alien religions and ideologies. Nor does it provide any protection against reading the interpreters' preconceived biases into the biblical passages they are interpreting. For example, in the late nineteenth century, Victorian Christians tended to read their own biases about the inferior "place" of women into biblical passages like Ephesians 5 in ways that overstepped the original intent, context, and meaning of those biblical "household codes," which were originally meant to clarify how women, men, and all Christians were to function within their respective conventionally ordered social contexts.

In 1988, Pope John Paul II amended such one-sided views about subjection of the wife in his apostolic letter *Mulieris Dignitatem* (On the Dignity and Vocation of Women). Reinterpreting the statement, "Wives, be subject to your husbands, as to the Lord. For the husband is the head of the wife" (Ephesians 5:22-23), the pope insisted on *mutual* subjection of spouses as a "gospel innovation" by Christ. "The author [of the Letter to the Ephesians] knows," the pope explained, "that this way of speaking, so profoundly rooted in the customs and religious tradition of the time, is to be understood and carried out in a new way: as a *'mutual subjection out of reverence for Christ'* (cf. Ephesians

5:21)."[12] In this case, theological and historical criticism work together to provide an accurate reading of the passage.

Misuse of Biblical Terms in Dispensationalist "Rapture" Theories

A more recent example of a misapplication of scriptural terms and passages, which has several similarities to the ways in which the earliest Gnostics misused Scripture, is the phenomenon of dispensationalist theories of the "rapture" (the simultaneous transport to heaven of all believers upon Christ's "first" return) exemplified in the best-selling Left Behind series of novels by Tim LaHaye and Jerry B. Jensen.[13] The term "dispensation" refers to a plan or a system of promises, and is used in a passage in Ephesians in reference to the end of time: "That in the dispensation of the fulness of times he might gather together in one all things in Christ, both which are in heaven, and which are on earth; even in him" (1:10, King James Version). The ancient Gnostics had been able to find scattered biblical verses and terminology that they could "mix and match" into an entirely novel and alien mythological system incompatible with Scripture's revelation and message. Similarly, the dispensationalist authors of these novels have been able to combine passages, verses, and biblical terminology that were originally scattered through biblical books as diverse as Ezekiel, Daniel, 1–2 Thessalonians, the gospels, and Revelation into their non-biblical theory of two independent "dispensations" or scenarios of the end times, in which Christ returns before and after a time of tribulation.

Dispensationalists claim that the old promise of a Messiah to Judaism (found in the Old Testament) is *yet to be fulfilled*:

for example, Ezekiel's new Temple is still waiting to be built in a new Jerusalem. This literalist reading fails to account for Revelation's unambiguous reinterpretation of Ezekiel, which is definitive for Christians, in which *there will be no new Temple in the new Jerusalem* (Revelation 21:22). As the gospels also expressed it, Jesus substituted resurrection of the temple of his body for construction of a new Temple in Jerusalem.[14]

Such elaborate dispensationalist timelines and scenarios of the end times, of which there are several competing and irreconcilable versions, are not found in the principal teachings about the end times revealed through the canon of Scripture taken as a unity. Moreover, they are clearly incompatible with biblical revelation about the end times. Without taking verses and passages completely out of their natural scriptural contexts, there is no biblical warrant for a *rapture* of "good Christians" before the tribulations of the end times, which would have to be endured only by sinners and non-Christians. Nor does Scripture in its canonical entirety support more than one more return of Jesus (not a preliminary return to "rapture" Christians, but only his return at the last judgment to judge the world at the very end of time, as in Matthew 25:31-46).

Nevertheless, LaHaye and other dispensationalist theorists insist that they use almost exclusively biblical terminology and the messages of "Scripture alone." In fact, however, their use of Scripture has many similarities to how the Gnostics at the time of Irenaeus used the Bible—skimming many passages to extract verses or expressions that seem to support their preconceived theories. Such a reading of scattered biblical passages also does violence to the biblical context of much of the scriptural evidence they claim for their end-time scenarios and positions.

The elaborate theories about the end times that they construct from scattered biblical evidence are as alien from actual biblical eschatology or teaching about the end times as were Gnostic interpretations of Scripture. The elaborate dispensationalist scenarios about the end times constructed by LaHaye and others bear no more resemblance to biblical interpretation about the end times in most Christian denominations (not only Catholicism) than Irenaeus' Gnostic mosaic of a dog bore to the biblical mosaic of the king.

Conclusion

While avoiding the potential pitfalls of other patristic writers, Sts. Irenaeus and Athanasius responded to the heretical challenges of their time by using non-biblical language and the "rule of faith" to interpret Scripture passages within the story line of salvation. These methods enable us to read Scripture as Catholic Christians, in light of the New Testament, the teachings of the church, and advances in biblical scholarship. In hindsight, Christians know how God's Old Testament story of salvation is concluded—that is, in the reconciliation of alienated humans to God through the incarnation, death, and resurrection of God's Son. Therefore, it is no longer instinctive or typical for Christians to continue to read the Old Testament as if they were the original Hebrews who were ignorant all we have learned in the last two millennia. The use of theological interpretation, following the example of Irenaeus and Athanasius, also hold promise for challenging more modern literalist misreadings and other misapplications of Scripture.

Although theological criticism—particularly of the Old Testament—is more useful to Catholic Christians today than interpretations that focus exclusively on the meaning of Scripture passages for their original historical audiences, there nevertheless is value in sometimes trying to reread the Old Testament through the eyes of the original readers. Even though Christians may know "the ending of the story," they can come to a deeper appreciation of the richness of God's providential plan by attending to its intricate windings from its early stages with "fresh eyes." Therefore, at least in higher educational settings, there remains a place for a focus on "Hebrew Scriptures" for their original theological insights, without flattening out their distinctiveness from later Christian rereadings. Moreover, close attention to the original context of a passage is often crucial to correctly determining its meaning.

Still, this seems a matter of "both-and" rather than "either-or": ordinary Christians or students should not be forced to choose between reading and understanding the Jewish books "*either* as the Hebrew Scriptures *or* as the Old Testament." They might profit, however, from reading them "*both* as Hebrew Scriptures *and* as the Old Testament." Sts. Irenaeus, Athanasius, other church fathers, and medieval saints have modeled for contemporary Christians how to read biblical passages both very closely in themselves and with theological insight into their deeper meaning. They have shown us a way in which we can now read any particular passage in either the Old or New Testament just as closely and carefully as is currently expected in academic exegesis, but also within the theological context of God's overarching biblical story of salvation, which gives ultimate theological and spiritual meaning to every individual biblical passage.[15] Our next chapter will look more closely at the model that St. Irenaeus gives us of interpreting Scripture theologically.

Notes

1. Cf. Luke Johnson's Chapter Two, "Rejoining a Long Conversation," in Luke Timothy Johnson and William S. Kurz, *The Future of Catholic Biblical Scholarship: A Constructive Conversation* (Grand Rapids, MI: Wm. B. Eerdmans, 2002), pp. 35–63, which discusses and recommends consulting church fathers and precritical interpreters of Scripture. Because the Enlightenment period in the eighteenth century followed the bloodshed and devastation from the religious wars in Europe, it sought to replace by critical reason such irrational and destructive behaviors and beliefs that were generated by conflicting religious beliefs and denominations.

2. Roland Teske, "The Good Samaritan (Lk 10:29-37) in Augustine's Exegesis," in *Augustine: Biblical Exegete*, ed. Frederick Van Fleteren and Joseph C. Schaubelt, OSA (Augustinian Historical Institute Villanova University; New York: Peter Lang, 2001), pp. 353–57.

3. In addition, Paul's allegory drastically transposed the original referents of the biblical Ishmael and Isaac. It applied the biblical figure of Ishmael (considered the ancestor of the historical Arabs) to the Jews of Paul's day. On the other hand, it applied the Genesis figure of Isaac (ancestor of the historical Israel and the Jews of Paul's time) to Christians, who included former gentiles and pagans as well as Jews. Even when he used it, Paul's comparison of Jews to descendents from Ishmael was intentionally ironic, for he mentioned that Jews "born of the flesh" were persecuting Christians "born according to the Spirit": "But as at that time he who was born according to the flesh persecuted him who was born according to the Spirit, so it is now" (Galatians 4:29). Still, this reversal of biblical Ishmael and Isaac sounds even more ironic and disturbing today when recent and contemporary news releases have been highlighting conflict and even warfare between Arabs (from Ishmael) and Jews (from Isaac).

4. Christopher Seitz demonstrates that the kind of overall biblical narrative approach developed by the patristic authors has a grounding in the New Testament itself. Using especially Lukan examples, he illustrates how the expression "according to the Scriptures" situates the identity and mission of Jesus in the context of God's saving plan and actions recounted in the Old Testament. The gospels and fathers from the second and third centuries described Jesus by situating him in God's saving plan as revealed in their Scripture (Old Testament) combined with the apostolic witness to Jesus [before the completed "canonized" New Testament]. (Christopher R. Seitz, *Figured Out: Typology*

and Providence in Christian Scripture [Louisville, KY: Westminster John Knox Press, 2001], p. 104.)

Seitz also relates the patristic use of the *rule of faith* to this use of the Old Testament narrative of God's saving plan. Because for Christians the Son and Father are one, both Old and New Testaments provide a unified witness to them via the Holy Spirit (Seitz, 6). See Luke 16:31: "He said to him, —If they do not hear Moses and the prophets, neither will they be convinced if some one should rise from the dead." Cf. also Luke 24:27: "And beginning with Moses and all the prophets, he interpreted to them in all the scriptures the things concerning himself." Luke 24:44-49: "Then he said to them, 'These are my words which I spoke to you, while I was still with you, that everything written about me in the law of Moses and the prophets and the psalms must be fulfilled.' Then he opened their minds to understand the scriptures, and said to them, 'Thus it is written, that the Christ should suffer and on the third day rise from the dead, and that repentance and forgiveness of sins should be preached in his name to all nations, beginning from Jerusalem. You are witnesses of these things. And behold, I send the promise of my Father upon you; but stay in the city, until you are clothed with power from on high.'"

5. Cf. Robert Louis Wilken, "*In Dominico Eloquio*: Learning the Lord's Style of Language," *Communio* 24 (Winter 1997) 846–66, p. 863: "It [the rule of faith] began with the confession of God as creator, briefly narrated the coming of Christ, told of his suffering, death, and resurrection, the sending of the Holy Spirit, and ended by pointing to the return of Christ in glory. By presenting the story of the Bible in capsule form, the rule of faith or 'pattern of truth' defined the subject matter of the Bible, thereby offering a commentary on the whole."

6. *Irenaeus Against Heresies*, Book I, Ch. VIII.—How the Valentinians pervert the scriptures to support their own pious opinions: "Their manner of acting is just as if one, when a beautiful image of a king has been constructed by some skilful artist out of precious jewels, should then take this likeness of the man all to pieces, should rearrange the gems, and so fit them together as to make them into the form of a dog or of a fox, and even that but poorly executed; and should then maintain and declare that this was the beautiful image of the king which the skilful artist constructed, pointing to the jewels which had been admirably fitted together by the first artist to form the image of the king, but have been with bad effect transferred by the latter one to the shape of a dog, and by thus exhibiting the jewels, should deceive the ignorant

who had no conception what a king's form was like, and persuade them that that miserable likeness of the fox was, in fact, the beautiful image of the king. In like manner do these persons patch together old wives' fables, and then endeavour, by violently drawing away from their proper connection, words, expressions, and parables whenever found, to adapt the oracles of God to their baseless fictions." (*Ante-Nicene Fathers* [*ANF*], ed. Alexander Roberts and James Donaldson, rev. A. Cleveland Coxe [American reprint of Edinburgh ed.; Grand Rapids, MI: Wm. B. Eerdmans, reprinted 1969], Vol. 1, p. 326.)

7. Wilken, p. 862.

8. See Joseph T. Lienhard, *The Bible, the Church, and Authority: The Canon of the Christian Bible in History and Theology* (Collegeville, MN: The Liturgical Press [A Michael Glazier Book], 1995), pp. 49–52, esp. p. 51.

9. Wilken, 862, quotes Henri de Lubac: "Jesus Christ brings about the unity of the Scripture, because he is the endpoint and fullness of Scripture. Everything in it is related to him. In the end he is its sole object. Consequently, he is, so to speak, its whole exegesis" (citing *Éxégèse Médiévale* 1:322 [ET 1:235]).

10. Especially helpful as a guide to patristic biblical interpretation is Frances Young, *Virtuoso Theology: The Bible and Interpretation* (Eugene, OR: Wipf and Stock, 1993, originally published in England by Darton, Longman and Todd, Ltd., as *The Art of Performance: Towards a Theology of Holy Scripture*), ch. 3, "Tradition and Interpretation," pp. 45–65, and ch. 4, "Jewish Texts and Christian Meanings," pp. 66–87.

11. Thomas Forsyth Torrance, *Theology in Reconstruction* (Grand Rapids, MI: Wm. B. Eerdmans, 1966), p. 33: Torrance finds that theological statements are made by hard exegesis in light of the truth to which Scripture points. For Athanasius, the supreme example of exegetical and theological activity is the *homoousion* of Nicea. As a compressed statement, it becomes normative for all theological statement that is to be faithful to its proper object and consistent with other faithful statements.

See also p. 36: The epistemological significance of the Nicaean *homoousion* doctrine of consubstantiality of the Incarnate Word and Son of God "lies in the rejection of the Valentinian and Arian dichotomy that made the *Logos* in the last resort a creature of God . . . and lies in the insistence that in Jesus Christ we have a *Logos* that is not of man's devising but One who goes back into the eternal Being of God for he proceeded from the eternal Being of God. The Incarnation means that God has really given himself and communicated himself in his eternal Word to man."

Cf. Thomas F. Torrance, *Divine Meaning: Studies in Patristic Hermeneutics* (Edinburgh: T&T Clark, 1995), p. 253.

12. Pope John Paul II, "Apostolic Letter *Mulieris Dignitatem* of the Supreme Pontiff John Paul II on the Dignity and Vocation of Women on the Occasion of the Marian Year," § 24, accessed June 20, 2006 at http://www.vatican.va/holy_father/john_paul_ii/apost_letters/documents/hf_jp-ii_apl_15081988_mulieris-dignitatem_en.html (italics in original).

The pope demonstrates an awareness of how challenging this interpretation of mutual subjection is for many times and cultures. "The 'innovation' of Christ is a fact: it constitutes the unambiguous content of the evangelical message and is the result of the Redemption. However, the awareness that in marriage there is mutual 'subjection of the spouses out of reverence for Christ', and not just that of the wife to the husband, must gradually establish itself in hearts, consciences, behaviour and customs. This is a call which from that time onwards, does not cease to challenge succeeding generations; it is a call which people have to accept ever anew. . . .

"But the *challenge presented by the 'ethos' of the Redemption* is clear and definitive. All the reasons in favour of the 'subjection' of woman to man in marriage must be understood in the sense of a 'mutual subjection' of both 'out of reverence for Christ'. The measure of true spousal love finds its deepest source in Christ, who is the Bridegroom of the Church, his Bride" (§ 24, italics in original).

13. Tim LaHaye and Jerry B. Jenkins, *Left Behind: A Novel of the Earth's Last Days* (Wheaton, IL: Tyndale House Publishers, 1995) was the first volume in the series. *Glorious Appearing: The End of Days* (2004) was their final volume in that series, which sold over fifty million copies. In 2005 a series of prequels began appearing, the first being Tim LaHaye and Jerry B. Jenkins, *The Rising: Antichrist Is Born before They Were Left Behind* (Wheaton, IL: Tyndale House Publishers, 2005).

14. Revelation 21:22 clearly reinterprets Ezekiel's new temple: "And I saw *no temple* in the city, for *its temple is the Lord God the Almighty and the Lamb*" (emphasis added). Sayings of Jesus in the gospels had already prepared for this, for example, John 2:19-21: "Jesus answered them, 'Destroy this temple, and in three days I will raise it up.' The Jews then said, 'It has taken forty-six years to build this temple, and will you raise it up in three days?' *But he spoke of the temple of his body*" (emphasis added).

For fuller Catholic responses to the arguments and claims of dispensationalists and rapture theorists and of the Left Behind series, see Paul Thigpen, *The Rapture Trap: A Catholic Response to "End Times" Fever* (West Chester, PA: Ascension, 2001), and Carl E. Olson, *Will Catholics Be "Left Behind"? A Catholic Critique of the Rapture and Today's Prophecy Preachers* (San Francisco: Ignatius, 2003). At Paul Thigpen's request, I published an alternative Catholic reading of many of the same biblical passages used by dispensationalists and rapture theorists, but within the context of the overall biblical canon and Catholic traditions of scriptural interpretation—William Kurz, SJ, *What Does the Bible Say about the End Times? A Catholic View* (Cincinnati, OH: St. Anthony Messenger Press/Servant Books, 2004).

15. Especially valuable in a search for a more theological method have been the following essays in Stephen E. Fowl, ed., *The Theological Interpretation of Scripture: Classic and Contemporary Readings* (Malden, MA: Blackwell, 1997): Henri de Lubac, "Spiritual Understanding," pp. 3–25; David C. Steinmetz, "The Superiority of Pre-Critical Exegesis," pp. 26–38; and especially David S. Yeago, "The New Testament and the Nicene Dogma: A Contribution to the Recovery of Theological Exegesis," pp. 87–100.

Catholic contributions that overlap many of the concerns of *The Future of Catholic Biblical Scholarship* (perhaps more my emphasis than Johnson's) are Peter S. Williamson, *Catholic Principles for Interpreting Scripture: A Study of the Pontifical Biblical Commission's* The Interpretation of the Bible in the Church (Subsidia Biblica; Rome: Editrice Pontificio Istituto Biblico, 2001), and David M. Williams, *Receiving the Bible in Faith: Historical and Theological Exegesis* (Washington, DC: Catholic University of America Press, 2004).

CHAPTER 3

READING SCRIPTURE THEOLOGICALLY WITH ST. IRENAEUS

Reading the Bible theologically allows us to focus primarily on Scripture's spiritual message to us as twenty-first-century Catholic Christians. For Sts. Irenaeus and Athanasius, the motivation for developing a theological reading of the Bible was the misinterpretation and misapplication of Scripture by very influential biblical interpreters. Irenaeus' primary challenge was to counter the claims of the Gnostics, who used biblical stories and terminology in ways that misconstrued and sometimes even reversed their original sense and meaning. Guided by the church's "rule of faith," Irenaeus interpreted Scripture according to its salvation story line, which he traced through the Old and New Testaments. His "theological" interpretation is not without shortcomings, but provides a useful example for contemporary biblical interpretation.

Irenaeus' *Demonstration of the Apostolic Preaching*

Irenaeus is well known for his extensive writings *Against the Heresies* (henceforth, *Heresies*), which have survived in a complete Latin translation of the lost original Greek, and for a small book recently discovered in Armenian translation, *The Demonstration of the Apostolic Preaching* (henceforth, *Dem-*

onstration).[1] *Demonstration* summarizes the Catholic faith and characterizes this synopsis as the *truth found in the preaching of the apostles* (even though it was in fact extracted primarily from Scripture) and proven (or as the title verbalizes it, *demonstrated*) by the prophetic writings (Old Testament). In his introduction to *Demonstration*, Irenaeus actually uses the phrase, "rule of faith," in telling his readers, "we must keep the rule (*canōn*) of faith unswervingly, and perform the commandments of God, believing in God and fearing him, for He is Lord, and loving Him, for He is Father" (*Demonstration* § 3).[2]

The education of most ancient and patristic writers was based on Greco-Roman rhetoric. In their book, *Sanctified Vision: An Introduction to Early Christian Interpretation of the Bible*, John J. O'Keefe and R. R. Reno explain that Irenaeus borrowed the terms "hypothesis," "economy," and "recapitulation" from classical rhetoric. Rhetorical theory called the gist or point of a work its hypothesis. According to Irenaeus, the main problem with heretical interpretation of Scripture is that it ignores the primary hypothesis of the Bible. While focusing on details and symbols, it fails to show how "the beginning, middle, and end hang together." For Irenaeus, the hypothesis of Scripture is that Jesus fulfills all things. "Economy" refers not to anything monetary but to the proper sequence, arrangement, or organization of a work. (The term originally referred to the management of a household.) God's economy is his timetable, schedule, or plan of salvation. Later generations tended to prefer the expression "salvation history" to the patristic word "economy." An ancient rhetorical "recapitulation" is a work's final summing up, repetition, and drawing to a conclusion. In oratory it refers especially to the summary at the end of a speech that drives home the point of its strongest arguments. For Irenaeus, Jesus is the Father's summary statement, his Logos or Word. According to Irenaeus' interpretation of Scripture, Jesus came according to God's "economy" and "recapitulated"—or brought to fruition—everything in himself.[3]

Irenaeus' *Demonstration* (written before A.D. 200) provides an extremely early and concise example of a theological approach to Scripture that extracts from the Bible an overarching biblical narrative of God's creation and salvation of the world. As Irenaeus' personal summary of the biblical salvation narrative, *Demonstration* exemplifies some of the interpretive principles and strategies that came to predominate in Catholic theological biblical interpretation through the patristic and medieval eras, and which growing numbers of contemporary Catholic biblical scholars are trying to revive in forms that are appropriate for today. In fact, his *Demonstration* is one of the earliest surviving summaries of Christian teaching that is neither polemical nor apologetic. It is a pastoral writing by a bishop that is intended as a "catechetical treatise" for his people.

In is important to note, however, that Irenaeus' *Demonstration* is not written in "catechism" form. It is modeled upon the apostolic preaching exemplified in the New Testament itself by the speeches in the Acts of the Apostles. Rather than summarizing abstract doctrines, Irenaeus' catechesis recounts God's saving actions, which culminate in the exaltation of his incarnate and crucified Son and in the bestowal of the Holy Spirit. Like the Acts of the Apostles, but contrary to contemporary expectations, this summary of apostolic preaching is grounded more deeply in the Old Testament than in the New, even though Irenaeus also knew the New Testament writings.

Demonstration is a striking reminder and illustration of how for Irenaeus and the early church, even the "apostolic preaching" (which by A.D. 200 was also available in written form in books of the New Testament) is grounded in the authority of the Old Testament Scriptures. (And, of course, the Hebrew Scriptures, which Christians now call the Old Testament, were the only completed Scriptures available to Jesus himself and to the first apostles in their early preaching.) That is, from the beginning, Christian claims that Jesus was Messiah and Savior were presented in apostolic preaching and later in New Testament writings as fulfillment of Old Testament expectations and as proof from Old Testament prophecy.

By comparing Old Testament expectations, reasons, and explanations of God's plan of salvation with events from the life, death, and resurrection of Jesus, the Acts of the Apostles and the letters of St. Paul validated the claim that salvation came through Christ. What was written in the Old Testament was exemplified and fulfilled in the words and deeds of Jesus, to which the apostles were the original and primary witnesses. In other words, apostolic preaching and catechesis combined interpretation of the Old Testament with living witness by the apostolic generation about Jesus.

Irenaeus maintained this pattern of emphasizing Old Testament demonstrations of Jesus' messiahship even after the apostolic witnesses were available only in written form, in the books of the New Testament. Irenaeus, however, differed significantly from theologians today because he could still claim living links with the actual preaching of the apostles. He plausibly claimed to have received the Catholic faith directly from disciples of the original apostles (*Demonstration* § 3).

Demonstration on the Faith of the Church

Irenaeus' summary treatment of Catholic faith begins with reference to baptism "for the remission of sins, in the name of God the Father, and in the name of Jesus Christ, the Son of God [who was] incarnate, and died, and was raised, and in the Holy Spirit of God,"[4] which seals us for rebirth and eternal life as sons of the eternal God. Because God created everything, he, therefore, rules everything as almighty Lord. Irenaeus begins his narrative proper with God's act of creation (*Demonstration* § 3–4).

In treating creation, Irenaeus uses a quasi-philosophical demonstration that bears some similarities to St. Thomas' thirteenth-century philosophical proofs for the existence of God as first cause of the universe. Irenaeus argues that all things that come into being must have "received the origin of their being . . . from some great cause; and the origin of all is God, for He Himself was not made by anyone, but everything was made by Him" (*Demonstration* § 4).[5] This one God created the world.

Therefore, there is only one God, the Father, Creator of all, above whom and after whom there is no other God. Because God is rational and verbal (*logikos*), he created by his Word [*Logos*]. Because God is spirit, he adorned (*kosmeō*, cf. cosmos) all things by his Spirit. Irenaeus bolsters his claims that creation was from both Word and Spirit by citing Psalm 32:6 (LXX, Psalm 33:6) "*By the Word of the* LORD were the heavens established, and all their power *by his Spirit*" (emphasis added).[6] Irenaeus refers to the author of this psalm as "the prophet," imitating New Testament references to David as prophetic author of the psalms who prophesied the Messiah in them (as in Acts 2:30-31).

Irenaeus is here unpacking the meaning of biblical texts in manners similar to those used within later Old Testament writings and in the New Testament, and in works by early Jewish rabbis and Christian church fathers. Often loosely referred to as "midrashic" by analogy to Jewish *midrash* (i.e., interpretations and applications of Scripture that go beyond the obvious immediate literal meaning and reference of the words), these interpretations applied ancient Scriptures to contemporary situations. Irenaeus argues in midrashic fashion that since Psalm 32 indicates that the Word "establishes" or gives form and existence, and that the Spirit arranges the powers, that, therefore, the Son is rightly called the Word, and the Spirit is called the Wisdom of God (*Demonstration* § 5). Although most early Christian writers apply both "Word" and "Wisdom" to the Son, Irenaeus' distinction between Son as Word and Spirit as Wisdom is consistent with his references to the Word and Spirit as the two "hands of God."[7]

After presenting God's creating activity, Irenaeus summarizes the "order of our faith," which also grounds our conduct by serving as its foundation. The *first article* of our faith is "God, the Father, uncreated, uncontainable, invisible, one God, the Creator of all." The *second article* is "the Word of God, the Son of God, Christ Jesus our Lord, who was revealed by the prophets . . . according to the nature of the economies of the Father." The Son "in the last times, to recapitulate all things, became a man amongst men, visible and palpable, in order to abolish death, to demonstrate life, and to effect communion between God and man." (The themes of God's *economy* or plan of salvation and the *recapitulation* of everything by Christ are two mainstays of Irenaeus' theological interpretation of Scripture.)

The *third article* of faith is the Holy Spirit, "through whom the prophets prophesied . . . and who, in the last times, was poured out in a new fashion upon the human race renewing man, throughout the world, to God" (*Demonstration* § 6).[8]

Therefore, in baptism we receive "regeneration unto God the Father through His Son by the Holy Spirit: for those who bear the Spirit of God are led to the Word, that is to the Son, while the Son presents [them] to the Father, and the Father furnishes . . . incorruptibility" (*Demonstration* § 7).[9] Irenaeus' treatment of the Trinity culminates in what God (the Father, Son, and Holy Spirit) intends for us humans—*incorruptibility*, or our sharing after death in God's everlasting life. This is closely related to a major theme of the early fathers, *theosis* or *divinization*—that *God became man so that man could be divinized* to become like God.

St. Athanasius would later express it thus, "He, indeed, *assumed humanity that we might become God*."[10] Although the theme of divinization has been more prevalent in eastern than in western regions of the church, it was still prominent in the West in the thirteenth century, as demonstrated by St. Thomas Aquinas' reflections on the feast of Corpus Christi. "Since it was the will of God's only-begotten Son that men should share in his divinity, he assumed our nature in order that *by becoming man he might make men gods*."[11] A contemporary and far better known western example is a prayer in every Roman Liturgy of the Eucharist at the offertory preparation of gifts. When the priest or deacon pours wine and a little water into the chalice, he says, "By the mystery of this water and wine *may we come to share in the divinity of Christ who humbled himself to share in our humanity*."[12]

Adam had been created in the "image and likeness" of God (Genesis 1:26), but had lost his original likeness to God by disobediently trying to "be as God" himself (Genesis 3:5). Through his resurrection from death, the incarnate Son of God restored to humans the possibility of endless godlike life with God. What Adam had arrogantly tried to seize against God's will, namely *divinization*, Jesus has mercifully restored and granted to us. Through God's compassion, we can share God's divine life (beginning even now through our new life from baptism). After death we can be resurrected, glorified, and made immortal and capable of heavenly union with God.

The patristic theme of divinization may be at least partly a logical development from the New Testament teaching that Christians are made "children of God" (e.g., John 1:12; Romans 8:16-21; Philippians 2:14-15; 1 John 3:1-2; cf. 5:1). Irenaeus' summary describes the relationship between God and Irenaeus' three religious categories of human beings (Jews, gentiles [pagans], and Christians) in the following manner: The Father is called "Most High," "Almighty," and "Lord of Hosts," because God is "the Creator of angels and men, and the Lord of all, by whom all things exist, and from whom all things are nourished . . . the God of all—both of the Jews and the Gentiles and of the faithful" (*Demonstration* § 8).

For Christians, God also has a more intimate title than "Almighty" or "Lord of Hosts": "However, to the faithful He is as Father, since 'in the last times' He opened the testament of the adoption as sons" (*Demonstration* § 8). Irenaeus explains that to the Jews of the Old Testament, God was known as "Lord" and "Lawgiver" in order to educate and bring alienated humans back to him; whereas, to the gentiles, he was known as "Creator" and "Almighty." But for everyone, Jews, gentiles, and Christians, God is "Nourisher, . . . King, and Judge, for no one shall escape

His judgement [sic], neither a Jew nor a Gentile, neither a sinful believer nor an angel" (§ 8).[13]

Demonstration on the Fashioning and History of Man

Irenaeus' paraphrase of the biblical account of the creation and fall of humans primarily summarizes the Genesis narratives. He includes some midrashic embellishment of Genesis to try to explain why Eve (and, consequently, Adam) was so easily led astray by the serpent's temptation. He suggests that Adam and Eve were created as naive children to explain both why they were so easily misled and why they were not ashamed of their nakedness.[14]

Against heretical disparagement of matter and the human body, Irenaeus emphasizes God's use of earthly material to fashion man's body in Genesis 2, as well as man's creation in the image and likeness of God (Genesis 1:26-28), so that humans would have freedom and could be commissioned by God to rule over the other material beings (*Demonstration* § 11). As did both the Wisdom of Solomon and Revelation, Irenaeus links the tempting serpent of Genesis 3 with Satan, but he adds the midrashic interpretation that the serpent had been possessed by Satan and that God cursed both the serpent and Satan dwelling within it (§ 16).

Irenaeus continues his midrashic paraphrase of Genesis by briefly referring to the spread of sin and God's punishments and salvation. He mentions the stories of Cain and Abel, the discovery of witchcraft, and Noah. Regarding the three post-flood human bloodlines, he stresses the curse on Ham (ancestor of the Canaanites who were displaced by the Israelites) and the blessing on Shem and Japeth (ancestors of Semites, who include Israelites, and of Hellenistic gentiles, respectively) before discussing Babel (*Demonstration* § 17–23).

After extremely sketchy highlights about Abraham, Isaac, Jacob (Israel), Moses, the desert generation, Deuteronomy, and the promised land (from Joshua through David, Solomon, and the Temple, *Demonstration* § 24–29), Irenaeus mentions the prophets as immediate preparation (§ 30) for God's saving intervention in the incarnation (§ 31–34). Irenaeus emphasizes that the Holy Spirit admonished the people through the prophets and heralded the coming of Jesus Christ, the Son of God, from his pre-existing with the Father until his "being revealed to all the world at the close of the age as man, 'recapitulating all things' in Himself" (§ 30).[15]

In recounting the incarnation, Irenaeus emphasizes that the incarnate Son "united man with God and wrought a communion of God and man." Otherwise, we would be unable to partake in God's *incorruptibility*. As we were all implicated in the creation of Adam, the source of our race, and were all bound to death through Adam's disobedience, we were all released from death through the obedience of the incarnate one.

"So, 'the Word became flesh' that by means of the flesh which sin had mastered, . . . it [sin] might be abolished and no longer be in us." The Lord received the same embodiment (*sarkōsis*) as Adam in order that he might conquer in Adam the very source in Adam of our affliction (*Demonstration* § 31).[16] Irenaeus emphasizes that Christ's *flesh* is the means by which we attain incorruptibility, in order to counter heretical claims that originally humans were purely spiritual divine sparks (and, therefore, incorruptible) but became trapped in alien material, corruptible bodies (which are, therefore, not really intrinsic to our being).

To explain the virgin birth, Irenaeus emphasizes that the beginning of humankind took place in Adam's being fashioned from the "virgin" earth. The Lord Jesus *recapitulated* Adam (became the new Adam) in receiving a similar arrangement (*oikonomia*, "economy") of embodiment (*sarkōsis*) "from the Virgin by the will and wisdom of God, that He might . . . become the man, written in the beginning, 'according to the image and likeness of God'" (*Demonstration* § 32). Adam was recapitulated in the Lord, who had come to seek the lost sheep—human beings. Similarly, was Eve recapitulated in Mary, "that a virgin, become an advocate for a virgin, might undo and destroy the virginal disobedience by virginal obedience" (a very early example of the Eve–Mary comparison, § 33).

Irenaeus goes on to assert that the obedience of Jesus in dying on the tree of the cross undid the original disobedience occasioned by the tree in the garden (*Demonstration* § 34). This fulfilled the promise to Abraham, making the gentiles and Christians righteous not by the law but by faith (Habakkuk 2:4; Romans 1:17; Galatians 3:11), as testified in the Law and Prophets (cf. Romans 3:21). The incarnate Son also fulfilled the promises to David that a king from his descendants would have an eternal reign (2 Samuel 7:12-13; Psalm 131:11; Acts 2:30 in § 35–36).

Irenaeus next emphasizes that the birth, death, and resurrection of the Son were genuine events. If one does not accept Christ's birth from a virgin, he asks, how can one accept his resurrection from the dead? (*Demonstration* § 37–39).[17] It is by communion with the Son that we humans can participate in incorruptibility (§ 40). The last section of the first part of *Demonstration* provides a quick summation of the argument to that point, reviewing how Christ was proclaimed by the law through Moses and witnessed by his apostles (§ 41). The apostles established the churches and invited the gentiles, whom Irenaeus midrashically identified as the descendants of Japeth who received Japeth's blessing (Genesis 9:27), namely that they would dwell in the "house of Shem" (i.e., share in Semitic Israel's covenant blessings as members within the church, which is now the "house" of God's people).

The second half of *Demonstration* provides a "demonstration from the prophets" that events relating to Christ that were impossible for nature were foretold by the prophets about our salvation (§ 42). *Demonstration* § 43 claims that Moses and Jeremiah (and John's prologue) prophesied that the Son existed "in the beginning" with the Father. The next paragraphs cite Moses (Genesis) as reporting that the Son (called LORD in Genesis 18:1-3) spoke with Abraham as one of Abraham's three visitors (the other two being angels) and threatened Sodom with punishment (§ 44), and that the Son related to Jacob (§ 45) and spoke to Moses from the bush (§ 46).

Therefore, Irenaeus concludes (*Demonstration* § 47) that both the Father and the Son are identified as Lord and God by Moses. According to their being (*hypostasis*) and essence (*ousia*), the Father and Son are one God. Yet, according to the plan (*oikonomia,* "economy") of our salvation, there is both Father and Son. It is through the incarnate Son that we have access to the invisible Father. Also, David (Psalm 45:7-8) refers both to Son and to Father as God, and says that the Son is anointed by the Holy Spirit.

In *Demonstration* § 48–66, Irenaeus cites further Old Testament prophecies by David (in the Psalms), Isaiah, Moses (in the Pentateuch), and others that function as divine foretelling of the identity, circumstances, and nature of the incarnate Son. David says that the Son is Lord in Psalm 110 (§ 48). Irenaeus explicitly designates Isaiah and David, traditional author of the Psalms, as "both prophets," asserting that Isaiah (45:1) and David (Psalm 2:7) call him Son and King of nations (§ 49). Isaiah (42:1 and 49:5-6) also refers to the Son as Servant (§ 50). Irenaeus mentions that it was the pre-existing Son of God whom the Father addressed as Servant in these same passages (§ 51).

Irenaeus further claims that Isaiah (7:14-16) foretold that a virgin shall conceive the incarnate Son and he shall be known as *Messiah* (the *Christ* anointed by the Father, Isaiah 61:1/Luke 4:18); *Jesus* (the *Savior* who would heal humanity from sicknesses, raise us from the dead, and bring us to eternal salvation); and *Immanuel* (revealing the good news that "He, being God, is going to be with us," *Demonstration* § 53–54).[18] In § 55, Irenaeus explains that Isaiah (9:6) calls the Son Wonderful Counselor, claiming that the Father addressed the statement "Let us make man" to the Son as his Wonderful Counselor.

Irenaeus cites several more prophecies: by Moses (Genesis 49:10-11) that the Son would be a ruler from Judah; also by Moses (Numbers 24:17) about a star from Jacob, which he relates to the star in Matthew's infancy narrative; by Isaiah (chapter 11) that the Son would be a rod from the root of Jesse and that at his *parousia* (second coming) he would bring peace even among warring nations and among such animals as a lion and lamb (*Demonstration* § 59–61). God also prophesied through Amos (9:11, cf. Acts 15:16) that he would raise the fallen hut of David through the resurrection of the body (viewed as a tabernacle, § 62); through Micah (5:2) that the Christ would be born in Bethlehem, David's homeland (§ 63); through David (Psalm 132:10-

12) that his Son would rule forever (and "forever" is true only of Christ, § 64); and through Isaiah (Isaiah 62:11 combined with Zechariah 9:9) that the Christ would come to the daughter of Zion (=Jerusalem) on the foal of an ass (§ 65). In § 66 Irenaeus summarizes this section of prophecies, claiming that they foretell how the Son would be begotten and where he would be born, and that he is Christ, the only eternal king.

Demonstration on Jesus' Ministry and Miracles, His Passion, and His Glorification

Finally, Irenaeus lists Old Testament prophecies regarding Jesus' ministry and miracles, his passion, and his glorification (*Demonstration* § 67–85). Isaiah foretold the miracles, passion, and resurrection of Christ: he would be scourged and killed for our sins (§ 67–68); by his wounds we would be healed; he would suffer in silence as a lamb, and in his abasement our judgment would be taken by him instead of by us who deserved it (§ 69). Who would declare his lineage? Because it was from the Father, it would be unknown to us (§ 70).

Isaiah and David prophesied Christ's resurrection from the dead to take on incorruptibility: the phrase "he lay down and slept and arose" (Irenaeus' paraphrase of Psalm 3:5) was symbolic of his death and resurrection (*Demonstration* § 72–75). Prophecies of further details of Jesus' suffering, death, and descent into hell are cited from Zechariah, the twelve prophets, Jeremiah (apocryphal), Isaiah, David, and Moses (§ 76–82). Irenaeus finds Old Testament prophecies of Jesus' ascension into heaven and his entering the gates of heaven as King of glory. He emphasizes the contrast between the Word's ascension into heaven as incarnate and visible and his earlier descent from heaven as invisible Word. Now he sits at the right hand of the Father (§ 83–85).

The last major set of prophecies that Irenaeus itemizes relates to the calling of the gentiles to become the new people of God (*Demonstration* § 86–97). He asserts that the witness of the apostles to Jesus was foretold by the prophets, who wrote that out of Zion (Jerusalem) the law would go out to all the earth. Isaiah prophesied that a "concise word" would summarize the law: Paul and Jesus both specified that this one word that fulfills the law is "love." The Lord himself saved the people because he loved them. Therefore, "Remember not the former things," because God is making something new and pouring out his Spirit. Jeremiah made clear that this was to be a new covenant.

Isaiah, Hosea, and Ezekiel prophesied that the new covenant would be inherited by the gentiles, who had not previously sought God. God would call those who were not his people "my people," and would put into them a new heart and a new Spirit (*Demonstration* § 86–93). Irenaeus ends his overview of Old Testament prophecies with reminders to his gentile converts to rejoice as the barren wife who has now borne children. He reminds them that God is using a formerly foolish people (pagan gentiles) to make his Old Testament people jealous (Romans 11:11-15) and that Christians no longer need the law as pedagogue (custodian or guide, Galatians 3:24-26), because only in the name of the Lord Jesus are people saved. They are to give thanks to God for bringing God's wisdom from heaven to them (§ 94–97).

Irenaeus' demonstration concludes by repeating that this is the preaching of the truth of our salvation, announced by the prophets, confirmed by Christ, and handed over by the apostles to the church, who passes it on throughout the world to her children. Readers are not to think "that there is another God the Father besides our Creator, as the heretics think." Others "despise the advent of the Son of God and the economy of his incarnation, which the apostles handed over and the prophets foretold would be the recapitulation of mankind." Still others "do not admit the gifts of the Holy Spirit, and cast off the prophetic grace from themselves." Thus, error has caused many to stray from the truth, either through despising the Father, rejecting the Son and the plan of his incarnation, or rejecting the Holy Spirit by despising prophecy (*Demonstration* § 98–100).[19]

The Example of Irenaeus: Limitations and Lessons

Like Irenaeus in his *Demonstration of the Apostolic Preaching*, contemporary biblical scholars can extract from Scripture the fundamental narrative of God's creation and salvation of the human race. Biblicists today can also profit from the example of the patristic and later pre-critical interpreters of the Bible, including even New Testament authors, who put extraordinary emphasis on the first three chapters of Genesis as a summary of foundational truths about the creation and the fall. Like Irenaeus, we can cull summaries of important steps in God's plan for our salvation from the Old Testament and find their climax and turning point in the incarnation of the Son of God, the Second Person of the Blessed Trinity.

Nevertheless, some of Irenaeus' midrashic explanations and applications, although generally clever and based on rather close and insightful reading of details in the biblical texts, have not stood the test of time and sound a bit quaint to contemporary ears—e.g., that Adam and Eve were created as naïve children, easily deceived and unashamed of their nakedness (*Demonstration* § 12, 14). Scholars today can often improve on Irenaeus' interpretations because we have the example, writings, experience, and insights of church fathers and believers in the centuries since Irenaeus. History and science have also made enormous legitimate advances since around A.D. 200, when *Demonstration* was written, and have filled in and explained many gaps and details in biblical passages. Nevertheless, we can admire Irenaeus' pastoral zeal and careful and insightful reading of Scripture, while conceding his occasional mistakes and idiosyncrasies.

Conclusion

Against Gnostic perversions and misuse of biblical language to support their entirely non-biblical ideologies and mythologies, Irenaeus had to insist on situating disputed expressions and passages within the church's tradition and understanding of the overall message of Scripture. Today the church needs new interpreters like St. Irenaeus to expound Scripture theologically in response to contemporary concerns and questions. Like Irenaeus, theologically oriented biblical scholars today will find themselves consulting the church's rule of faith when interpreting Scripture to make sure that passages are not abused in ways that are utterly alien to its main messages. Like Athanasius, as we shall see in the next chapter, they may well have to find appropriate contemporary philosophical ways to express core biblical teachings in response to contemporary philosophical denials of the possibilities of those teachings.

Notes

1. See Behr's introduction, pp. 7–8, in *St. Irenaeus of Lyons*, On the Apostolic Preaching, trans. & intro. John Behr (Crestwood, NY: St. Vladimir's Seminary Press, 1997).

2. Behr, p. 41.

3. John J. O'Keefe and R. R. Reno, *Sanctified Vision: An Introduction to Early Christian Interpretation of the Bible* (Baltimore: Johns Hopkins University Press, 2005), pp. 35–38.

4. Behr, p. 42, original parentheses.

5. Behr, p. 42.

6. The abbreviation LXX stands for *Septuagint*, a term for the Greek translation of the Old Testament. The numbering of most of the Psalms differs in the Septuagint (and the Latin Vulgate Old Testament translation) from the numbering in the standard Hebrew text. Here Psalm 33 in the Hebrew and in English translations is numbered Psalm 32 in the Septuagint and Vulgate.

7. See Irenaeus, *Against Heresies*, Book 4, Preface § 4: "Now man is a mixed organization of soul and flesh, who was formed after the likeness of God, *and moulded by His hands, that is, by the Son and Holy Spirit,* to whom also He said, 'Let Us make man'" (Gen. 1:26, in Roberts, Alexander, James Donaldson, and A. Cleveland Coxe. *The Ante-Nicene Fathers Vol. I: Translations of the Writings of the Fathers Down to A.D. 325. The Apostolic Fathers With Justin Martyr and Irenaeus.* Oak Harbor: Logos Research Systems, 1997, ECF 1.1.7.1.4.1, italics mine); also in *Ante-Nicene Fathers* (note 11), Vol. 1, p. 463.

Cf. Irenaeus, *Heresies*, Book 5, Chap. 28, § 4: "And therefore throughout all time, man, having been moulded at the beginning *by the hands of God, that is, of the Son and of the Spirit*, is made after the image and likeness of God" (italics mine, in *ANF*, Vol. 1, p. 557).

Cf. Irenaeus, *Heresies*, Book 4, Chap. 20, § 1: "For God did not stand in need of these [beings], in order to the accomplishing of what He had Himself determined with Himself beforehand should be done, *as if He did not possess His own hands. For with Him were always present the Word and Wisdom, the Son and the Spirit, by whom and in whom, freely and spontaneously, He made all things,* to whom also He speaks, saying, 'Let Us make man after Our image and likeness'" (italics mine, in *ANF*, Vol. 1, pp. 487–88).

8. Behr, pp. 43–44.

9. Behr, p. 44. Bracketed word in original.

10. *St. Athanasius on the Incarnation: The Treatise* De Incarnatione Dei, trans. & ed. a religious of CSMV, w. intro. by C. S. Lewis (Crestwood, NY: St. Vladimir's Orthodox Theological Seminary, rev. 1953, reprint 1982) § 54, p. 93 (emphasis added). Thomas Torrance summarizes Athanasius' teaching on implications of the incarnation thus: "For he was made man (*enanthrōpēsen*) that we might be made divine (*theopoiēthōmen*) and he manifested himself through a body (*dia sōmatos*) that we might receive a conception (*ennoian*) of the invisible Father" (Torrance, *Divine Meaning*, ch. 7, "Athanasius: A Study in the Foundations of Classical Theology," 179–228, 187). (I transliterated the Greek letters quoted by Torrance.)

Cf. a somewhat related notion in St. Ambrose, "Concerning Virgins, to Marcelina, his Sister," Book 1, Chap. 3, § 11: "Then a Virgin conceived, *and the Word became flesh that flesh might become God*," *ANF* (via "The Early Church Fathers from the original 38 Volumes by Harmony Media, Inc" [a CD], italics mine). The way that other humans besides the incarnate Word are divinized is through their union with and membership in the Body of this incarnate Word.

11. From St. Thomas Aquinas, *Opusculum 57, in festo Corporis Christi*, lect. 1–4, quoted in *The Liturgy of the Hours: According to the Roman Rite*, trans. ICEL (New York: Catholic Book Publishing Co., 1975), 3:610.

12. *The Vatican II Weekday Missal* (Boston, MA: Daughters of St. Paul, 1975), 848, emphasis added.

13. Behr, pp. 44–45.

14. *Demonstration* § 12 & 14. John Behr mentions other early fathers who use this theory, but how Ephrem of Syria [308?–73] came to label the idea "pagan" (Behr, 104, n. 39).

15. Behr, p. 60.

16. Behr, pp. 60–61.

17. Behr, pp. 64–65.

18. Behr, p. 75.

19. Behr, pp. 100–1. There is some disagreement about whether sections 99–100 of this conclusion were original with Irenaeus or added later to apply the *Demonstration* to a polemic against Gnosticism (*Demonstration*, p. 118, n. 229).

READING SCRIPTURE THEOLOGICALLY WITH ST. ATHANASIUS

In several ways, St. Athanasius advances theological interpretation of Scripture further in the direction on which Irenaeus had set out. He is closer to Irenaeus than to Catholic interpreters from his city of Alexandria who had preceded him, Clement and Origen, who were more inclined to the use of allegory. As would be expected, the challenges and heretical interpretations that Athanasius faced were different from those to which Irenaeus had responded more than a hundred years earlier. As a result, some of the methods Athanasius used to counter their arguments differed from those employed by Irenaeus, as well.

Many Gnostic arguments and interpretations from Scripture would instantly strike most Christians as strange and alien to their beliefs. Arians, however, tended to base their arguments on seemingly plausible interpretations of biblical passages that, at first reading, seem to support their version of the faith. Arians were not disposed to take these biblical passages and statements as thoroughly out of their natural biblical context nor to distort their obvious meaning as fully as the Gnostics had done. Arians regarded themselves, rather, as teaching authentic Christian doctrine, whereas Gnostics were more openly providing an alternative religion and version of reality.

Athanasius, therefore, usually took the Arian arguments

from biblical passages quite seriously and respected their plausibility enough to reevaluate these passages anew. In accordance with the primary message of Scripture and of Christian belief in God's saving action in the incarnation, Athanasius reinterpreted the very passages that the Arians had used as "proof-texts" to support their heretical denials of the divinity of the Son and Word. Because the controversies were particularly focused on whether the Son was created or divine, Athanasius' arguments had to reckon with topics related to philosophical metaphysics or ontological questions about what kind of *being* the Son of God is. In his attempts to resolve philosophical questions about being, Athanasius could not limit his replies to the Arians to what he was able to express in biblical language. With the Council of Nicea, therefore, he championed the pivotal importance of an admittedly non-biblical philosophical terminology.

Expanding the Context of Biblical Interpretation

St. Athanasius, like many contemporary biblical scholars, insisted that Scripture had to be interpreted in reference to its *context*. Significantly, though, he broadened the notion of context to include not just the immediate context of a passage but the entire Bible and the doctrine of our faith. On the level of the Bible itself, Athanasius interpreted Scripture in terms of "the scope of biblical usage," i.e., its purpose in its original context. In terms of the relation of the Bible to objective reality, however, Athanasius interpreted Scripture according to "the scope of faith or doctrine," i.e., its theological purpose or its purpose within the context of church doctrine or faith.[1] This is similar to use by fathers like Irenaeus of the church's rule of faith as a context for understanding any individual biblical passage.

When Athanasius determined the scope or intent of biblical usage, his method was similar to those of contemporary biblical scholars, namely learning Scripture's characteristic patterns of speech and argument. This requires the reader to observe on what occasion, by whom, and to whom the passage was written, and what issues and concerns it was written to address. This is quite comparable to what contemporary scholars do in studying the historical or human meaning of Scripture.[2]

But Athanasius went beyond most contemporary academic interpretation of Scripture when he investigated not only "the scope of biblical usage" but also proceeded to interpret Scripture within "the scope of faith or doctrine." This explicitly theological kind of interpretation of Scripture seeks out what the biblical passages mean and to what they refer. It requires not only studying what is written in the biblical books but "the acts of God to which they bear witness—i.e., to the whole economy of salvation . . . of the Incarnate Son of God." Therefore, biblical interpretation has to be theological and remain within the scope of Catholic faith and its fundamental doctrines. Biblical statements and terms are interpreted by weighing their human language within the pattern of God's saving plan.[3] Their true meaning is grounded in the Word, or Son of God in his divine and human natures and the atoning (saving) purpose of his incarnation. Guiding our biblical interpretation by the scope of Scripture and the scope of faith thus grounds our biblical understanding and theological statements directly on Jesus Christ.[4]

For Athanasius, therefore, interpretation must account for the *context* of every passage, especially its immediate context.

"This implies a rejection of tropological and allegorical exegesis," which often distort the text's natural sense or misapply it.[5] But interpretation must also consider the larger context of the whole scope of the scriptural writings according to their customary expressions and subject matter and to the religious experience they mediate. Thus, biblical interpretation consults the apostolic mind and the church's experience and faith.[6]

Expanding the Vocabulary of Biblical Interpretation

Because Arian denials of the Son's divinity used biblical language and were supported by citations of biblical passages, Athanasius could not merely repeat the same biblical terms and language to argue that Jesus is divine. Instead, he employed more explicitly theological terminology to express more accurately and with less confusion the realities to which the biblical passages referred. Some of the biblical statements and passages that Arians were quoting in a proof-texting manner to support their false teaching were also taken out of context, at least out of the fuller canonical context of the complete Bible. So, Athanasius grounded his interpretation in the broader scope of the narrative of salvation.

Arians justified their refusal to acknowledge that Jesus is God on the basis of the human language that Scripture is forced to use to speak about God/Jesus. Their arguments were based on the customary human meanings of biblical language—for instance, that because Jesus is God's "son," he must have had a beginning, as all human sons do when generated by their fathers.

Athanasius contended that human language was often inadequate to describe God. When words such as "son" were applied to God, they had to be understood as having meanings that differed from their everyday human meanings. Another way to put it is that they had to be understood metaphorically, because they referred not to an ordinary human being but to God.

Thus, when the word "son" is applied by Scripture to the Son of God, the generation implied by the human term cannot be applied without change in its meaning to God's divine nature, which transcends the limits of human language. A human father necessarily exists before generating his son, who comes into existence only later and only through his father's causality. In God, however, the Father is eternally generating the Son, who is co-eternal to the Father, and is equally God as the Father is God. Thus, an Arian overemphasis on literal biblical language could in reality amount to a misuse of biblical terms and passages in order to promote their misleading human doctrinal systems, which undermined the common Christian faith.

Interpreting this language within the scope of faith, Athanasius argued that biblical words such as "son" have to be interpreted differently from the ordinary meaning those terms have. Furthermore, since Jesus is the Son of God, Arians should not quibble about expressions that Scripture applies to the Word, for they apply to him according to his nature as incarnate Son of God rather than according to the ordinary meaning of the terms. In other words, Scripture is to be interpreted by the "apostolic mind," by what the apostles taught. Thus, biblical language about the Son has to be understood within "the limits of the Gospel . . . and the fulfilled economy [plan]. . . of the Incarnation."[7]

Arians also based their argument that Jesus was not divine on biblical verses that seemed to imply that the Word of God was *created* by God. With many Christian interpreters, they equated Wisdom in Proverbs 8:22-23 with the Word, or Son, of God: "The LORD *created me at the beginning of his work,* the first of his acts of old. Ages ago I was set up, at the first, before the beginning of the earth." Their next step was to argue that if the Son was created, even if he was created first to be the instrument for creating all other creatures, he could not himself be divine. In response, the bishops at Nicea had to scramble to find more fundamental, even philosophical, terminology that could distinguish plainly between *the Son as begotten* and *a creature as made.*

The Nicene fathers also needed precise ways to rebut the closely related Arian insistence that there was a time when the Word did not exist. If the Son ever began to exist, as Arians argued from Proverbs 8:22 and similar biblical statements, he could not possibly be of the same divine essence or being as the Father. Logically, he would have to be a creature made by the Father who existed before he did, as Arians asserted.

The wording chosen at the Council of Nicea was admittedly non-biblical, but the bishops claimed that it was able to represent faithfully the underlying significance of the biblical evidence.[8] They defined the Son as *homoousios,* of the same being or essence as the Father. He was "the only Son of God, eternally begotten of the Father, God from God, light from light, true God from true God, begotten, not made, of one Being with the Father."[9]

If the Word or Son is of the same being as the Father and co-eternal with the Father, then Arian arguments from passages like Proverbs 8:22, that the Word was created and did not exist before then, would violate the context of the scope of faith, within which Athanasius argues that the passage has to be interpreted. For Athanasius, if the Word is God, then the Word cannot have been created, as the Arian reading of Proverbs 8:22 implies. When faced with the apparent contradiction from the clear use in Proverbs of the phrase "created me," Athanasius tried to avoid applying that phrase to the pre-incarnate Word or Son by using the broader scope of faith to apply it rather to the human nature of the Son become incarnate, which indeed was created. This allowed Athanasius to insist, despite the apparent meaning of Proverbs 8:22, that the divine nature of the Son was not created. Later I will indicate some problems with his solution and suggest an alternative.

For Athanasius, the incarnation is the link between the eternal divine nature of the Word or Son and the created human nature of Jesus. Jesus is not only *like God,* he *is God.* In the incarnation, God "has himself entered his creation," so that from the incarnate Son we can now truly understand divine things. In the incarnation God both reveals himself to us and saves us by restoring us to union with himself. It was for our sake that the Son appropriated our human nature.

Like church fathers before him, Athanasius emphasized that when humans, in fact, did reject God and his commands in trying themselves to be as God, no mere finite human creature could repair that human offense against God's infinite dignity. As both God and man, only the incarnate Word was in a position to be able to mediate between God and man and to reconcile them.

As both God and man, the incarnate Word is also the only human source of knowledge of the unlimited being of God, who in his infinite being exceeds the reach of unaided limited human knowledge.[10] When Arians denied the divinity of the Son, or

Word, and placed the Son among the ranks of creatures, they were eliminating the basic prerequisite for Christ's mediatorship and atoning reconciliation between God and man.

Athanasius remained instinctively convinced that the reason God created man was so that man might know and love God, since he was related as rational *(logikos)* creature to God through his Word *(Logos)*. We can truly know God, though, only from a source or principle in God himself and according to God's works and ways of revealing himself. The source that God has provided for us to know him is the incarnate Word of God, who is the only *outward appearance* of the invisible Godhead. Therefore, only from him as Word of God can any true knowledge of God be attained. If the Word is not of the same being and substance as God *(homoousios)*, he cannot reveal to us who God is in himself, and, therefore, human speech about God is reduced to merely human speculations about God.[11]

There are two essential aspects to St. Athanasius' position. First, Jesus Christ is not a man somehow promoted to divinity, but he is the eternal Son and Word of God who stooped down, or "condescended," to become one with us in order to lift us up to God. Second, Jesus is not merely an instrument that God brought into being to meet a human need, he is the reality of the Father's eternal Word. Even as incarnate, he is consubstantial with the Father. God "condescended" to our ignorance so that we might know the true God. In his incarnate life, Jesus has enabled our knowledge of God.[12]

The two doctrines of the *condescension* of the eternal Word to man and the *consubstantiality* of the incarnate Word with the Father govern biblical and theological language about God for Athanasius. God's image in the incarnate Word comes from

God himself, not from human speculation. "*It is not an image external to God but internal to him, and rooted in his own Being.* It is the consubstantial image and Word that is manifested and revealed in Jesus Christ."[13] Only in Jesus can humans really know God the Father (Luke 10:22).

Problems in biblical interpretation arise from the conflict between God's ways of portraying himself to us through biblical writers and our ways of imaging God from our human preconceptions. We have to penetrate to the meaning of biblical language and not interpret only the surface expressions. The meanings of human expressions are modified when they refer to divine nature of the incarnate Son of God.

Therefore, in controversies, Athanasius did not resort to mere proof-texting from Scripture. For *proof* of Christian doctrines, it was not enough for him to appeal to biblical texts. He needed to look at what the Scriptures signified and at the acts of God to which they refer. The resulting theological language that Athanasius and the bishops at Nicea developed to explain these realities has served as a guide to further interpretation of the Bible.

Biblical Proof and Biblical Mystery

Athanasius had to admit, as we do, though, that inevitable difficulties will remain in interpreting the Bible, primarily because God's being infinitely transcends and surpasses our capacities for knowledge. Biblical statements concern *mysteries* that arise from the divine realities themselves, rather than from the words that are used in the Bible to describe them. The Arians claimed that the biblical terms and expressions themselves are mysterious and without meaning. But to do so is to "explain away" Scripture by transferring obscurity from the infinite nature of God to the necessarily human words used to describe his mystery.

For Athanasius, no human language can adequately express the mysteries of God. We should simply follow biblical language as far as it takes us, according to its function as God's self-revelation to us, which is expressed in language that we can understand with the help of the Spirit. The incarnation reminds us of two truths: that with our own unaided powers we are unable to know God, but also that through the incarnation we can have genuine knowledge of God. True interpretation uses a consistent set of theological statements that express the interior logic of the biblical message.[14]

After the Council of Nicea had disclosed the basic logic of the Christian faith, Athanasius insisted that a definitive groundwork for understanding Scripture had been laid, from which it is not reasonable to go back. The Nicean insight floods many biblical passages with significance and opens the way for much deeper understanding of Scripture. When in a genuinely religious manner we let our thoughts be formed by what God tells us in Scripture and let our minds be opened to God's self-revelation, and then reflect rationally on their message, we are engaging in what Athanasius means by hermeneutics, or biblical interpretation.[15]

The Example of Athanasius: Limitations and Lessons

St. Athanasius had to respond to Arian literalistic arguments from biblical passages that seemed to imply that the Son, or Word of God, was a creature (even if first to be created, as we have seen in the Arian interpretation of Proverbs 8:22, "The

LORD created me at the beginning of his work"). To be effective, his response had to get beyond the ostensible meaning of "created me" and situate the entire passage within the broader biblical context and message.

Athanasius began from the consensus of Arians and mainstream Christians alike that the personified Wisdom in Proverbs 8 was to be identified with the Word and Son of God (as in the prologue of the Gospel of John). He then made a theologically orthodox distinction (which is grounded in the context of the entire biblical canon) between the Word as pre-existent Son of God and the incarnate Word, or Son (Jesus).[16] Although this distinction is indeed grounded in the entire biblical canon read as a unity, it does not adequately address the sense of the explicit wording and context of Proverbs 8:22-23, which consensus held to refer to pre-existent Wisdom before creation of the world. The reference in Proverbs 8:22 to a pre-existent Wisdom figure remains an awkward anomaly that resists attempts by Athanasius to identify that figure with the *incarnate* Word.

Perhaps Athanasius' basic problem can be solved by using the prologue of the Gospel of John to interpret the otherwise seemingly unavoidable Arian-sounding use of "created" for Wisdom in Proverbs 8:22. A good argument can be made that John's prologue is reinterpreting not only the creation account in Genesis 1–2, but also the previous Hebrew interpretation of the Genesis account in Proverbs 8. Proverbs 8 had symbolically interpreted the creation account by *personifying* the wisdom by which God created this magnificent universe and emphasizing that God's wisdom existed before anything in the material universe was created.

Apparently to preserve the monotheism of Hebrew belief when

Proverbs was written, this personification of creative wisdom had been clearly distinguished from any possible second god by postulating its creation before all other creatures as the instrument that God used in creating the world. Perhaps Proverbs might be understood as also safeguarding the utter transcendence of the Creator God over all his creation. By portraying wisdom as an intermediate instrument of divine creation, Proverbs 8 could be said to picture the transcendent God creating the universe in a way that appears to "keep God's hands from getting dirty" by too intimate involvement in the act of creation.

Nevertheless, once Christians identified the personified Wisdom in Proverbs 8 with the Word, or Son of God, there were obvious and serious theological complications in such traditional Hebrew reinterpretations of the Genesis creation account. The Arians capitalized on these problems, and their interpretations had some justification, at least according to their literalist reading of that passage. The Greek translation of Proverbs 8:22, on which John's gospel was probably reflecting, uses the word "created" in "The LORD created me at the beginning of his work." The next verse, Proverbs 8:23, uses the Greek expression "*I was founded* [*my foundation was laid*]" for the English "I was set up" (as the RSV translates verse 23): "Ages ago *I was set up*, at the first, before the beginning of the earth" (emphasis added).

Perhaps John's prologue deliberately retraces the reinterpretive steps taken by the Hebrew interpretation of creation in Proverbs. John 1 begins by making the same claim for the Word that Proverbs 8:22 had made for Wisdom. John 1:1-3 insists that the Word existed "in the beginning," and that "all things were made through him" (therefore he existed before creation, as Proverbs 8 had also asserted). Also, like Proverbs 8 for Wisdom, John 1 claims that the Word "was in the beginning with God," and further that "all things were made through him, and without him was not anything made that was made."

In a clear departure from Proverbs 8, John 1:1 further insists that "the Word *was* God," which seems to be a Christian theological clarification (or even a correction necessitated after Christians had identified the Son with Wisdom) of Proverbs 8, "The LORD *created me* at the beginning of his work." The Word who existed before the world's creation in John, whom most interpreters, both at the time of Athanasius and today, regard as equivalent to the Wisdom who existed before material creation in Proverbs 8:22, is clearly asserted to *be God, not created by God.*

In other words, one can read John 1 as a Christian adjustment and even correction of the possibly misleading implications of personified Wisdom in Proverbs 8 as later identified with the pre-existent Word or Son of God. Once one reads Proverbs 8 through the corrective reinterpretation of John 1, there is no longer need, at least by a contemporary interpreter, to resort to Athanasius' application of Proverbs 8 to the *incarnate* Word, which ultimately fails to do justice to the evident meaning of the Proverbs passage. This contemporary explanation would still fall within Athanasius' belief in God's plan as providing the ultimate context for any particular passage, including Proverbs 8.

This explanation deals with the theological problem in a different way, however, by simply showing how the New Testament passage in John provides a needed theological clarification and correction of possibly misleading language about Wisdom in Proverbs 8. This also corresponds to a general contemporary awareness that God's plan is *progressive* revelation, in which, during later stages of human development and divine revelation, God can clarify earlier passages that, when read literalistically, might be misleading.[17]

Thus, Proverbs 8 fulfilled an important and sound theological function when it was written, which later expanded. When the figure of Wisdom, who had initially merely personified the wisdom with which the one God created the universe, was equated by Christians with the pre-existent Word and Son of God, the literal wording of Proverbs retained some senses that could become misleading in later theological contexts. Such misleading connotations were explicitly corrected by still later reinterpretations of both Genesis 1 and Proverbs 8 by Christians, as in John 1:1-3. This contemporary explanation uses valid insights from recent scholarship to provide a context of development within biblical teachings from the time of Proverbs to the New Testament about the reality of the One but triune God who created the universe by his Word (and Son), who was both "with God" and who himself "was God" (John 1:1).

Conclusion

Despite the limitations in Athanasius' reading of Proverbs 8, he has nevertheless made significant contributions to a more theological interpretation of Scripture. By stressing the need to read Scripture by attending to both its immediate context and its broader biblical context and meaning within the narrative of salvation, he has expanded the scope of biblical scholarship. Moreover, he has called attention to the limitations of human language to capture the mysteries of the divine and to the subsequent need to read biblical language metaphorically in reference to its subject matter, which is grounded in the incarnation of the Word and the logic of God's plan for our salvation. When we attempt to unlock the meaning of God's story in Scripture—which was written with a divine purpose but expressed by a human author in human language and in a particular historical context—we would do well to follow Athanasius' example.

Notes

1. Cf. Thomas F. Torrance, *Divine Meaning: Studies in Patristic Hermeneutics* (Edinburgh: T&T Clark, 1995), ch. 8, "The Hermeneutics of Athanasius," 237. Among several helpful scholarly treatments of Athanasius' biblical interpretation, I have found this book by patristic scholar Thomas Torrance to provide the overview and analysis that can most easily provide an understandable summary of the main points of Athanasius' long treatises against the Arians.

2. Torrance, pp. 237–38.

3. Torrance, p. 273.

4. Torrance, pp. 240–42, with nn. 57 and 65. Because *tradition* has been handed down from Christ through the apostles and the church until his time, Athanasius regards it as identical to apostolic tradition and as equivalent to the content of Scripture. Jesus combines his command to baptize in the name of the Trinity with his promise to remain with the disciples (as *Immanuel*, "God with us"). Because Jesus remains with the apostles in their teaching, Athanasius identifies the actual content of the tradition with Jesus himself. "The written form of the tradition, the Holy Scripture, must be taken to 'speak out of the person of God'" (Torrance, p. 243). Therefore, the tradition can be received and passed on not by "demonstration of words" (as by the Arians), but only by faith and by "godly and reverent reasoning" (Torrance, p. 243). Only from within this tradition of the Catholic Church can readers grasp the true meaning of biblical terms as they refer to God, in distinction from their profane meanings or human opinions about them (Torrance, p. 244).

5. Torrance, p. 272. "Tropological" refers to finding the morally edifying sense of a biblical passage.

6. Torrance, pp. 272–73. J. D. Ernest reviews the way Athanasius utilizes the "scope of Scripture," a summary narrative about the Word from his preincarnate existence with the Father as Word and Son, through his incarnation and mission, to his present coexistence with Father as Lord (J. D. Ernest, "Atha-

nasius of Alexandria: The Scope of Scripture in Polemical and Pastoral Context," *Vigiliae Christianae* 47 [1993] 341–62 [extracted from *PCI Full Text*, ProQuest], 343–44). This *scope* becomes for Athanasius both his criterion and consequence of correct interpretation of Scripture. Use of this scope amounts to placing oneself within the biblical story (with the help of summaries of the plot such as the *regula fidei*, "rule of faith," and creeds).

7. Torrance, pp. 238–40.

8. Cf. Torrance, p. 253: "The *homoousion* is thus a supreme example of a strict theological statement arising out of the examination of biblical statements, derived by following through the ostensive reference of biblical images, and giving compressed expression, in exact and equivalent language, not so much to the biblical words themselves but to the meaning or reality they were designed to point out or convey. Once established it served as a further guide to the Scriptures, although, of course, it continued to be subordinate to the inspired teaching of the Apostles and to what the Church learned from the Scriptures which mediated it."

9. Nicene Creed, English Language Liturgical Commission translation, http://www.creeds.net/ancient/nicene.htm, last accessed March 14, 2006.

10. Torrance insists that Athanasius rejected the more philosophical understandings of the Word, including those by predecessors in Alexandria like Origen. He garnered his understanding of the Word from Scripture itself in light of the church's rule of faith, and he thus bypassed some of the overtones of Platonic philosophy that fed into allegorical interpretation of Scripture by Origen and others.

11. Torrance, p. 248.

12. Torrance, pp. 249–50.

13. Torrance, p. 251.

14. Torrance, pp. 285–86.

15. Torrance, pp. 287–88.

16. See Frances M. Young, *Biblical Exegesis and the Formation of Christian Culture* (Peabody, MA: Hendrickson Publishers, 1997, reprinted 2002), ch. 2, "The Mind of Scripture," 29–45 (on Athanasius vs. Arians), esp. p. 33 and pp. 37–45 (on exegesis of Proverbs 8:22).

17. This teaching about God's Old Testament revelation as being progressive and tailored to the people's developing awareness, which matured over time from primitive to more sophisticated theological conceptions, is supported by *Catechism* § 51–73.

CHAPTER 5

READING OLD TESTAMENT PASSAGES THEOLOGICALLY

This chapter will illustrate lessons learned from Sts. Irenaeus and Athanasius about *how* we can read passages from the Old Testament as Catholic Christians rather than as secular academics or as a reconstructed ancient "original audience." Though it is necessary to understand the original meaning and contexts of a passage, the message of Scripture for later readers in different contexts is often not fully identical with what that passage meant to its original audience. Nor does it make much sense for contemporary Catholic Bible readers to pretend that they can only derive from an Old Testament passage what ancient Israelite hearers or readers would perceive in that passage, and not read that passage with awareness of the revelation of Christ.

Irenaeus and Athanasius have demonstrated that one way to read the Bible as Christians is to read each biblical book or passage in the context of Scripture's overall biblical message and narrative of salvation, as well as in the context of the church's rule of faith and dogmatic teaching. Our generation radically differs, however, from both of these premodern church fathers in that we live in a postmodern, twenty-first-century world whose views are radically unlike ancient outlooks. One positive aspect of our altered situation is that we have inherited from modern biblical criticism some newer productive ways to reconstruct the original meaning of Scripture in its initial linguistic and cultural context.

As twenty-first-century Christians, we are, therefore, in a position to learn valuable lessons both from the writings of our early patristic forerunners and also from our contemporary approaches to the Bible. This chapter will illustrate theological interpretation of two story lines in the Old Testament: the story of the creation and fall of humanity in Genesis 1–3 and the story of salvation through the suffering Servant in Isaiah 52:13–53:12. Chapter 6 will examine some New Testament examples.

Reading the Story of Creation and the Fall as Christians Today

Patristic and medieval authors (and even the author of John's gospel) considered and treated the early chapters of Genesis as absolutely foundational for the biblical narrative of God's saving actions.[1] Both ancient and contemporary interpreters have put particular emphasis on Genesis 1–3. Many patristic and medieval church fathers have written commentaries on the *Hexaemeron*, that is, commentaries on "the six days of creation" in Genesis.[2] There seems to have been a decided consensus among patristic and medieval Christian writers that the early chapters of Genesis are vital for understanding the environment within which the first humans—and later generations—found themselves, both before and after the original human rebellion against the authority of their Creator.

Let us, therefore, begin our theological reading of a sample of Old Testament passages with Genesis 1–3. Following the example of the church fathers, our primary goal will not exclusively be to reconstruct the original way that the passages would have been understood by early Israelites, but to read them also with a conscious awareness of our contemporary Catholic beliefs and worldviews. Nevertheless, we cannot simply "read into" the passages our current preconceptions. We still have to grasp the meaning of the words themselves as they were first written. In other words, we will read Genesis 1–3 in an inclusive "*both-and*" manner, *both* determining the historical sense of the words in their original contexts, *and* understanding the theological message they contain as introducing the entire Catholic biblical canon.

In the Beginning—Creation from Nothing

"In the beginning God created the heavens and the earth" (Genesis 1:1).[3] The opening phrase in the Hebrew Bible, "In the beginning" (*beReshit*), and in its Old Greek translation (*en archē*), occasioned numerous ancient and medieval reflections and comments by both Jewish and Christian interpreters. In the Hebrew Bible, "In the Beginning" even became the title by which the book of Genesis was known.

The opening words of the Gospel of John consciously echo this phrase that starts the Bible: "*In the beginning* was the Word, and the Word was with God, and the Word was God. He was in the beginning with God; all things were made through him, and without him was not anything made that was made" (John 1:1-3). This Johannine prologue emphasizes that God created absolutely everything by his word (or Word) alone, as implied in Genesis 1:3 (and God's other creating commands), "And God said, 'Let there be light'; and there was light."

Reading this initial sentence of Genesis theologically, let us ask what is meant by "in the beginning." Most New Testament writers and earliest patristic interpreters based their interpretations on the Greek, which has a double meaning. Because *archē* in Greek can denote both a *beginning* in time and a *principle* that gives coherence and meaning to the whole, "in the beginning" in Greek suggested both the start of everything and also the wise ordering involved in God's creating the world.[4]

The key to the interpretation of the first three verses of Genesis for both early Israelite and Christian readers was the report of God's command in the third verse, "'Let there be light,' and there was light." In contrast to creation myths among the Israelites' pagan neighbors, God was not portrayed as forming the world from pre-existing matter. God began creating by his word alone. Nor was creation of this world portrayed as the result of some divine battle among several gods or between gods and pre-existing monsters. "In the beginning God created the heavens and the earth." God simply and effortlessly created all the known universe, which is summarized in the phrase "the heavens and the earth."

According to this classical interpretation, verses 2-3 go on to describe the initial condition of the *earth* that God created, along with the heavens, in verse 1. "The earth was without form and void, and darkness was upon the face of the deep; and the Spirit of God was moving over the face of the waters. And God said, 'Let there be light'; and there was light." God proceeds to bring order (over a "six-day" sequence) to the initial watery chaos he had created in the first verse, but with none of the struggle found in other ancient creation myths that existed at the time the Genesis story was told. Rather, God simply gave commands, and each kind of creature came into existence. Here, God merely spoke his word of command, "Let there be light." The result was immediate: "and there was light."

Already in the Hebrew Bible, passages like Psalm 33:6 (Psalm 32:6 in the Septuagint and Vulgate) have interpreted Genesis 1: 1-3 as God's creating by his mere word alone. "*By the word of the LORD* the heavens were made, and all their host *by the breath of his mouth*" (emphasis added). In the Hebrew poetic parallelism that is characteristic in the psalms, the second part of this verse paraphrases the first part, but from a slightly different perspective. The first half proclaims that the heavens were made by the Lord's *spoken word* ("Let there be light," Genesis 1:3), which the second half paraphrases as "by the breath of his mouth."

Later, when Christians read this same psalm verse, they saw hints of their belief in the Trinity: the Lord God created by his Word (the Son, as explained in John 1:1-18). God's breath or Spirit was also involved in that act of creation. (In Hebrew and in the Greek and Latin translations, the word for "breath" is the same as for "spirit.") This reading was even more predictable because most Christians used either the Greek Old Testament (LXX) or the Vulgate or other Latin translations of this verse. Both the Septuagint, which was used by the New Testament, Greek patristic writers, and Greek-speaking churches (to this day), and also the Latin Vulgate, which was used by the Latin-speaking churches through and beyond the Middle Ages, translated Psalm 33:6 (numbered 32:6 in LXX and Vulgate) as "By the *Word* of the LORD the heavens were made firm, and by the *Spirit* of his mouth all of their power" (my translation and emphasis).

Psalm 33:6 is part of a psalm of praise of the Creator and Lord of creation. Alluding to Genesis 1:3, "Let there be light," Psalm 33:6 makes clear that God created by his spoken word ("*by the word* of the LORD . . . *by the breath of his mouth*"). Then Psalm 33:7 poetically summarizes Genesis 1:2-10, which had narrated how God had brought order to the earth's initial watery chaos: "He gathered the waters of the sea as in a bottle; he put the deeps in storehouses." The psalm's following two verses express awe at God's creation of the world by his mere word of command: "Let all the earth fear the LORD, let all the inhabitants of the world stand in awe of him! *For he spoke, and it came to be; he commanded, and it stood forth*" (Psalm 33:8-9, emphasis added). Therefore, the rest of the psalm indicates that God's people are to hope for salvation not from their own strength, but from the Lord. Nor is Psalm 33 the only hymn about creation based on Genesis 1. Psalm 104 also celebrates in poetic language God's creation of the world, as well as God's providential care of human beings and all creatures on earth.[5]

When one inquires into the philosophical or theological implications of the proclamation that God created the world by his word alone, it is a small further step to argue that God created the world not from pre-existent matter but from nothing (the classical Latin expression *ex nihilo*). Although these implications of the Genesis account are not stated in Genesis, they are explicitly asserted in 2 Maccabees 7:28 (second century B.C.), in the story of the mother pleading with her son before the culmination of his martyrdom: "I beseech you, my child, to look at the heaven and the earth and see everything that is in them, and recognize that *God did not make them out of things that existed*. Thus also mankind comes into being."[6] In short, even though the belief that God created the world out of nothing (*ex nihilo*) is not expressly mentioned in Genesis, it is explicitly stated within Old Testament Scripture in a Hellenistic Jewish reflection on Genesis in the second century before Christ. An explicitly theological interpretation of Genesis does not hesitate to move beyond original meanings of Genesis to include deeper theological meanings about "creation from nothing" arrived at by later reflection on the text, both in the Old and New Testaments and in reflections of the church fathers.

Creation of Man and Woman in God's Image

Besides God's creation of the world "in the beginning," the other most theologically fertile parts of this Genesis creation account concern the origin of the human race and the place of human beings within the created world. Certain peculiarities in the narrative occasioned intense speculation among both ancient Jewish and Christian readers. Primary among these oddities was the unexpected switch to the plural in the divine "discussion" preparatory to creating man. "Then God said, '*Let us* make man in *our* image, after *our* likeness; and let them have dominion over the fish of the sea, and over the birds of the air, and over the cattle, and over all the earth, and over every creeping thing that creeps upon the earth'" (Genesis 1:26, emphasis added).

The earlier creation of other living things had been reported in compressed summary fashion as simple divine commands that were immediately followed by the appearance of each creature. The account of the creation of human beings, in contrast, is prepared by a dramatic buildup. Not only does human creation occupy the climactic position in the narrative, but it is not described as a mere command that is summarily implemented. Rather, it is presented as following a "discussion" to prepare for the proposed creation of humans. The passage also strongly underlines how humans are related to God as God's image, how humans are unique among material creatures, and how humans are given authority over other material creatures.

"So God created man in his own image, in the image of God he created him; male and female he created them" (Genesis 1:27). The earliest interpreters, both Jewish and Christian, explained that what made man an image of God was not his body, for God has no body, but human freedom and intellectual knowledge, which animals and other material creatures lacked. Nevertheless, this verse makes clear that it belongs to the very essence of man to be a bodily creature, unlike purely spiritual angelic creatures. Central to being human is that humans are "male and female," which implies their physical interrelationship.

The creation accounts that portray humans as male and female in Genesis 1, and as Adam and his wife, Eve, in Genesis 2–3, trace the origin and spread of the human race back to an original married couple. The Old Testament will continue to emphasize the importance of marriage for the propagation and spread of the human race in their mission from God to exercise dominion over the entire earth, even after the destruction of most humans by the flood and the race's new beginning from Noah and his sons' families. The New Testament will further reinforce the bodily nature of humans by emphasizing the bodily resurrection of Jesus and the prospective bodily resurrection of those who will be saved by Jesus.

Contrary to "unisex" cultural trends that would minimize the significance of one's sexual identity, Scripture puts extraordinary emphasis on the complementary sexual identity of all human beings. Adam's and Jesus' masculinity and Eve's and Mary's femininity are at the core of who they are as humans, not something merely superficial or extrinsic to their personal identity as human. And Scripture shows an even stronger confirmation of the goodness of human identity as male and female images of God than it had for all previous creatures. Creatures on most lower levels received a simple approval by their Creator, "And God saw that it was good." But after creating, commissioning, and blessing humans as the finishing touches on creation, "God saw everything that he had made, and behold, it was *very good*" (Genesis 1:31a, emphasis added).[7]

If we are to read Genesis 1 as believers and not only as secular academicians or historians, we can learn much about its interpretation from the ways that earlier believers celebrated, praised, and worshiped God for the truths proclaimed in Genesis. According to the Latin saying *"lex orandi lex credendi"* (what people believe can be discerned from how they worship and pray), we can look to the way in which Israelites and Jews worshiped God to learn what they believed about God as Creator. Thus, Psalm 8 reinforces the sense of the nobility and exaltation of the human creature in a hymn of praise to God for man's creation that echoes many aspects of the creation account in Genesis 1:

When I look at thy heavens, the work of thy fingers,
the moon and the stars which thou hast established;
what is man that thou art mindful of him,
and the son of man that thou dost care for him?
Yet thou hast made him little less than God,
and dost crown him with glory and honor.
Thou hast given him dominion over the works of
thy hands;
thou hast put all things under his feet,
all sheep and oxen,
and also the beasts of the field,

the birds of the air, and the fish of the sea,
   whatever passes along the paths of the sea.
(Psalm 8:3-8)

The psalm praises God for the magnificence of creation and then expresses awe at the exalted place given to man, who otherwise seems so insignificant in comparison with all the heavenly bodies in the vast universe. It reiterates the commission that God had given humans in Genesis, to have dominion over all the material creatures on earth. It thus illustrates ways in which humans are in God's image, both as having dominion over other material creatures and also as "male and female," fulfilling God's mandate to "increase and multiply and fill the earth and subdue it."[8]

Human Disobedience and Alienation from God's Friendship

The second and more imaginative narrative of God's creation of human beings in Genesis 2 prepares directly for the report of human disobedience to their creator and dismissal from his presence in Genesis 3. It complements the first recounting of human creation in Genesis 1 by placing new emphasis on the interrelationship between man and woman as well as by preparing to account for the origin of evil. This second version of man's creation emphasizes how God took raw material from the earth to form the human body and then breathed into it "the breath of life."

"Then the LORD God formed man of dust from the ground, and breathed into his nostrils the breath of life; and man became a living being" (Genesis 2:7). Early Jewish and Christian readers associated God's breathing into man the breath of life with an added enhancement to human nature beyond the nature of animals, which God had also created from the ground but without breathing into them the breath of life. Recall that the Hebrew, Greek, and Latin word for *breath* is the same as for *spirit*. Only into man did God breath the *spirit* (later reflection will call it the human *soul*) that made man a living being.

God also made the other creatures alive, but Genesis does not mention that God gave them a spirit. "So out of the ground the LORD God formed every beast of the field and every bird of the air, and brought them to the man to see what he would call them; and whatever the man called every living creature, that was its name" (Genesis 2:19). Human naming of the animals was another sign of human superiority to them.

Genesis 2:8 and 2:15 mention that God planted a garden and placed Adam within it to take care of it. From the beginning, humans are portrayed as tending God's earthly garden, with permission to eat of any plants except the tree of knowledge of good and evil. "You may freely eat of every tree of the garden; but of the tree of the knowledge of good and evil you shall not eat, for in the day that you eat of it you shall die" (Genesis 2:16b-17). Only Adam was present to hear this divine prohibition. It was not until after giving him this command that God sought to make a partner (Eve) for Adam.

Adam examined and named all of the animals, but none of them was a fit partner for him. Finally, from Adam's own rib (rather than from the earth, which God had used to make Adam and the animals) God fashions a suitable companion and partner for him. "This at last is bone of my bones and flesh of my flesh; she shall be called Woman, because she was taken out of Man" (Genesis 2:23). The narrator then underlines the marital implications of this story. "Therefore a man leaves his father and his mother and cleaves to his wife, and they become one flesh" (2:24). At this creation of the first human couple, marriage is portrayed as an exceptionally exalted vocation. The union of man and woman is the closest possible union, two in one flesh.

Such an exalted view of marriage and of union between man and woman evidently does not correspond to historical human experience, but Genesis makes clear that God's original intention for marriage could hardly have been more elevated. The narrative proceeds to indicate how it was human rejection of God's plan and commands that led instead to a resulting degeneration of man-woman relationships and marriage. When human creatures used their unique rationality and freedom to reject God's authority over them, they not only lost their intimacy with God, their Creator, but they also severely damaged their marital relationships with their human partners. Their two-in-one-flesh union was perverted into a relationship of lust, domination, mistrust, and mutual blame.

As humans had rebelled against the authority of God, so in the natural world both animals and plants in turn rebelled against human authority:

> Cursed is the ground because of you;
>> *in toil* you shall eat of it all the days of your life;
> *thorns and thistles* it shall bring forth to you;
>> and you shall eat the plants of the field.
> *In the sweat of your face*
>> *you shall eat bread*
> *till you return to the ground,*
>> *for out of it you were taken;*

you are dust,

  and to dust you shall return.
(Genesis 3:17-19, emphasis added)

Humans even lost control over their own internal physical-spiritual makeup and became ashamed of their nakedness, which they tried to "cover up." They became subject to death (returning to the ground from which they were taken). In short, all the sufferings and evils of historical human existence are attributed to primeval misuse of human freedom and disobedience to man's Creator.

Ancient commentators, both Jewish and Christian, have remarked on the fact that the first temptation was directed not to Adam, to whom God had given the original commandment, but to his wife, Eve, who had not been present when the command was given. They have also noted a discrepancy between what God had commanded Adam and what Eve reported God to have said in her response to the serpent. "You shall not eat of the fruit of the tree which is in the midst of the garden, *neither shall you touch it*, lest you die" (Genesis 3:3, emphasis added to highlight Eve's addition).

In both Old Testament and New Testament writings, the serpent was explicitly identified with Satan, or the devil (see Wisdom 2:24; John 8:44; and Revelation 12:9 and 20:2). The Hellenistic Jewish "Wisdom of Solomon" (second or first century B.C.) unmistakably alludes to Genesis 3 and identifies the serpent with the devil. The context concerns the blindness of the wicked to the realities of life and death:

Thus they reasoned, but they were led astray,
for their wickedness blinded them,
and they did not know the secret purposes of God,
nor hope for the wages of holiness,
nor discern the prize for blameless souls;
for God created man for incorruption,
and made him in the image of his own eternity,
but through the devil's envy death entered the world,
and those who belong to his party experience it.
(Wisdom 2:21-24, emphasis added)

The Book of Wisdom here suggests that God's original intention in creating humans was that they not have to die. It even implies that one manner in which humans were in God's image was that they were designed to live forever. The serpent is identified with the devil, who out of envy tried to get the first humans to break God's command so that they would incur the punishment of death. Death is, therefore, the outcome of human disobedience to their Creator, to which the serpent (identified as the devil) had tempted Eve.

In the New Testament, both the Gospel of John and the Book of Revelation confirm this identification of the serpent with the devil with similar allusions to Genesis 3. In a dispute with Jewish leaders, Jesus charges, "You are of your father the devil, and your will is to do your father's desires. *He was a murderer from the beginning,* and has nothing to do with the truth, because there is no truth in him. *When he lies, he speaks according to his own nature, for he is a liar and the father of lies*" (John 8:44, emphasis added). The reference to the devil as murderer probably alludes to the devil's role both in humans' incurring the punishment of having to die, as well as in Cain's consequent murder of Abel in Genesis 4. The reference to the devil as "a liar and the father of lies" alludes to the serpent's lying temptation of Eve in Genesis 3.

Revelation explicitly identifies its dragon figure, which Michael and his angels had just expelled from heaven, as "that ancient serpent, who is called the Devil and Satan, the deceiver of the whole world" (Revelation 12:9). The allusions to Genesis 3 focus especially on how the devil or ancient serpent had deceived the whole world, beginning with his deception of Eve. In a different context, Revelation repeats its identification of the dragon with Satan: "And he seized the dragon, that ancient serpent, who is the Devil and Satan, and bound him for a thousand years" (20:2). Thus, by the time of Jesus and the New Testament, the serpent in the Genesis 3 account had already been interpreted as the devil or Satan, which elevated the temptation narrative beyond a primitive folk tale toward a more sophisticated theological explanation of the origin of evil.

Reading the Story of the Suffering Servant as Christians Today

For Christian readers, the same chapter of Wisdom that identified the serpent with the devil has also prefigured the coming role of God's incarnate Son, Jesus, as a just man who will suffer persecution and death from evil men for our sake. From the beginning of the church, Christians have also turned to Isaiah 52:13–53:13 for insight into the meaning of the traumatic suffering undergone by the Messiah. This "servant song" has helped them understand and appreciate both what Jesus' suffering meant and why he suffered as he did.

When early Christians read Wisdom 2 in light of their recent experience of the death and resurrection of Jesus, they found in it many foreshadowings of what would happen to Jesus. The chapter quotes the ironic rantings of evil people who take offense at the goodness of the just man, for it pricks their conscience regarding their own evil deeds:

> Let us lie in wait for the righteous man,
> because he is inconvenient to us and opposes our actions;
> he reproaches us for sins against the law,
> and accuses us of sins against our training.
> He professes to have knowledge of God,
> and calls himself a child of the Lord.
> (Wisdom 2:12-13)

The original Greek for "child" in the last verse also means "servant." This double meaning allows Christians to see in the final clause a reference to Christ in two senses—he calls himself a child, or *son*, of God and also an innocent suffering *servant* of God. Christians will also relate this latter sense of Christ as suffering servant of God to the suffering servant passages of Isaiah (e.g., Isaiah 52:13–53:12), which profoundly influenced Christian reflection on the meaning of Jesus' passion and death and, therefore, also affected the passion narratives that climaxed the four gospels.

Christian readers would also see other foreshadowings of the fate of Jesus in the continuing rants of the wicked in Wisdom 2: "He calls the last end of the righteous happy, and *boasts that God is his father*" (2:16b, emphasis added). The plans of the wicked to test the innocent man as they torture him may well have influenced details in the way some passion narratives describe Jesus suffering on the cross and being mocked by the bystanders:

> Let us test what will happen at the end of his life;
> for *if the righteous man is God's son, he will help him,*
> *and will deliver him* from the hand of his adversaries.
> Let us test him with insult and torture,
> that we may find out how gentle he is,
> and make trial of his forbearance.
> Let us condemn him to a shameful death,
> for, according to what he says, he will be protected.
> (Wisdom 2:17b-20, emphasis added)

When Christians read these lines today, they surely hear echoes of the passion accounts in the gospels. Matthew's version in particular may well have been influenced by this Wisdom passage:

> . . . and saying, "You who would destroy the temple and build it in three days, save yourself! *If you are the Son of God,* come down from the cross." So also the chief priests, with the scribes and elders, mocked him, saying, "He saved others; he cannot save himself. He is the King of Israel; let him come down now from the cross, and we will believe in him. *He trusts in God; let God deliver him now, if he desires him; for he said, 'I am the Son of God.'"* And the robbers who were crucified with him also reviled him in the same way. (Matthew 27:40-44, emphasis added)

Neither the Markan nor Lukan versions of this incident mention the references to "Son of God" or to trust in God who should deliver him, which in Matthew bear such a striking resemblance to the passage from Wisdom quoted above (Mark 15:19-32, Luke 23:35-39). As Matthew describes the same incident, he uses phrases from the Old Testament to bring out more of the meaning of what happened to Jesus.

Isaiah 52:14 emphasized the reality and horror of the suffering of God's servant by noting the astonishment of witnesses at how disfigured he appeared in his suffering. The servant's disfigurement was mentioned again in Isaiah 53:3 as related to his rejection: "He was despised and rejected by men; a man of sorrows, and acquainted with grief; and as one from whom men hide their faces he was despised, and we esteemed him not."

The context within which Christians read this description was their overarching biblical narrative of God's creation and salvation of humans. As human sin abounded, God's mercy abounded still more. This culminated in God's decision that the Son would himself become incarnate as man to rescue us from our sinfulness and alienation. This rescue did not take the form expected by many of God's people, namely, military victory over their human enemies. Rather, it involved overcoming humans' sins plus the Savior's taking on himself the just punishment that their sins deserved. This "servant song" in Isaiah, along with comparable passages especially in the prophets and psalms, provided Old Testament justification and evidence that the divine plan of salvation was atonement by God's incarnate Son, not victory in war.

This description in Isaiah's prophecy explained that the horrible suffering endured by God's Son and the people's Messiah was borne for our sakes and because of our sins:

Surely he has borne our griefs
    and carried our sorrows;
yet we esteemed him stricken,
    smitten by God, and afflicted.
But he was wounded for our transgressions,
    he was bruised for our iniquities;
upon him was the chastisement that made us whole,
    and with his stripes we are healed.
(Isaiah 53:4-5, emphasis added)

The crucifixion of the Christian Messiah, Jesus, had been a terrible shock to Jesus' followers. As they searched the Scriptures for what meaning this traumatic event might have, this prophecy enabled them to understand that Jesus suffered not because he was rejected by God, but because of our sins. He took on himself the chastisement that we deserved and made us whole. We were healed by his stripes.

As the earliest Christians read this prophecy in hindsight after Jesus' crucifixion and resurrection, it provided them further explanation for what happened to Jesus and why it happened the way it did. It also laid a more profound foundation for the Christian doctrine of atonement. "All we like sheep have gone astray; we have turned every one to his own way; and the LORD has laid on him the iniquity of us all" (Isaiah 53:6). The Old Testament Scriptures are filled with dreadful examples of how God's people repeatedly rejected God's ways and commandments and "like sheep have gone astray." Over and over again Scripture emphasizes that God's people "turned every one to his own way" instead of obeying God's commandments and ways of living. This prophecy portrays how God lays on his just servant "the iniquity of us all" so that the servant would atone for the people's sins. Christians reading this passage naturally see Jesus as this servant of God who makes atonement for our sins.

The prophecy adds details that relate to Jesus' refusal to complain when undergoing his passion:

> He was oppressed, and he was afflicted,
> yet he opened not his mouth;
> like a lamb that is led to the slaughter,
> and like a sheep that before its shearers is dumb,
> so he opened not his mouth.
> (Isaiah 53:7)

Other details are emphasized in the various gospel passion accounts, such as Jesus' burial by a rich man, Joseph of Arimathea: "And they made his grave with the wicked and with a rich man in his death" (Isaiah 53:9). Isaiah's prophecy also mentions that because "he makes himself an offering for sin" (53:10), God will vindicate him. However, the form that the servant's vindication takes can only partially apply to Jesus:

> Therefore *I will divide him a portion with the great,*
> and he shall divide the spoil with the strong;
> *because he poured out his soul to death,*
> *and was numbered with the transgressors;*
> *yet he bore the sin of many,*
> *and made intercession for the transgressors.*
> (Isaiah 53:12, emphasis added)

Luke's gospel, for example, mentions Jesus praying as he was crucified alongside two thieves or rebels, "Father, forgive them for they know not what they do" (Luke 23:34). The vindication of Jesus was beyond what this or most prophecies imagined, namely his resurrection from the dead.

Conclusion

These sample Old Testament passages were selected to illustrate ways in which contemporary Christian readers can interpret Old Testament passages in ways that go beyond what original Israelite readers might have heard or understood from them. They illustrate pivotal steps in the Old Testament story of God's creation of the world and salvation of humans after they rejected his commands in their attempts to "be as God" themselves. Reflections on Genesis in later Old Testament books had already prepared for the New Testament and early Christian interpretation of Genesis, and ultimately for the Catholic doctrines of creation from nothing (*ex nihilo*), original sin and the fall, and for the incarnation and atonement of the Son of God.

As Christians, we now can read the Bible as a unity based on its single authorship by God as the primary author who inspired the various human biblical authors. Even within the Old and New Testaments, we can read older and more primitive Old Testament passages with the help of later reinterpretations of those earlier writings. Even if later Christian dogmas are not fully expressed in Genesis and other Old Testament passages, the reinterpretations of Genesis in the Psalms, wisdom books, and prophets have filled in much of the gap between the original Old Testament account and later church doctrine. The New Testament reinterpretations fill in this gap between Old Testament account and Catholic doctrine even more.

If we are to read the Bible theologically as Catholics, we read older parts of the Bible in light of later biblical and church interpretations and explanations. We don't ordinarily settle for reading Scripture the way the original audience heard or read it, trying to imagine ourselves back in the situation of the original writing. Though this is a valuable academic exercise, we now can read Scripture with the greater fullness that comes from the entire biblical canon and Catholic traditions of interpretation. From early church fathers like Sts. Irenaeus and Athanasius, we can learn much about theological insight into biblical writings. From our contemporary training and situation, we can sometimes improve on what the early fathers were able to understand about the original meaning of the passages as they were written. Let us now turn to what it means to read the New Testament writings theologically as God's biblical word.

Notes

1. See William S. Kurz, *What Does the Bible Say About the End Times? A Catholic View* (Cincinnati, OH: St. Anthony Messenger Press, 2004), ch. 1, "In the Beginning: Genesis 1-3," pp. 7–27; Luke Timothy Johnson and William S. Kurz, *The Future of Catholic Biblical Scholarship: A Constructive Conversation* (Grand Rapids, MI: Wm. B. Eerdmans, 2002), ch. 7, "Beyond Historical Criticism: Reading John's Prologue as Catholics," pp. 159–81, esp. pp. 167–72, on the prologue's actualization of Genesis with special attention to the Greek version.

2. *Hexaemeron* (or *Hexameron*) is Greek for "six days" and refers to the six days of creation. E.g., see the discussion and bibliographical notes on the many patristic commentaries on the *Hexaemeron* in J. C. M. Van Winden, OFM, "In the Beginning: Some Observations on the Patristic Interpretation of

Genesis 1:1," *Vigiliae Christianae* 17 (1963): 105–21, accessed July 4, 2006, from JSTOR at http://www.jstor.org/view/00426032/ap050062/05a00040/0. See also Saint Ambrose, *Hexameron, Paradise, and Cain and Abel*, trans. John J. Savage (New York: Fathers of the Church, 1961).

Cf. also Gordon J. Wenham, *Genesis 1–15* (Word Biblical Commentary, Vol. 1; Nashville, TN: Thomas Nelson Publishers, 1987), p. xlv: "Though Christian theologians have devoted most of their attention to Genesis 1–11 or more precisely Genesis 1–3, the rest of the book has been comparatively neglected."

3. The biblical translation used will be the Revised Standard Version (RSV) unless otherwise indicated, partly because it is a reasonably literal translation that, when possible, uses the same English term for the same original Hebrew or Greek expression, and partly because it pre-dates more "politically correct" translations, which can obscure the Bible's original wording. In Genesis 1:1, the RSV translation is especially important for theological interpretation because it provides the standard English translation on which most traditional theology in English has been based. It is also helpful because it is both based on the Hebrew and also usually agrees with the ancient Greek and Latin translations of Scripture used throughout the church's history.

In contrast to this traditional opening of Scripture, which serves as the foundation for most Christian (and even Jewish) theology and worship, recent historically "purist" translations from Hebrew have been using alternatives that are proving to be theologically distracting. Thus the New American Bible (NAB), which is used in Catholic liturgies, reads: "In the beginning, *when* God created the heavens and the earth, the earth was a formless wasteland, and darkness covered the abyss, while a mighty wind swept over the waters" (Genesis 1:1-3, NAB). That translation is quite similar to most recent biblical translations and is a reasonable historical reconstruction of the sense of the original Hebrew.

It is not, however, particularly supportive of the classical interpretation of the vast majority of ancient commentators, namely that God created the universe *ex nihilo*, "out of nothing," by his word alone. That interpretation is already implied in Psalm 33:6, "By the *word* of the LORD the heavens were made, and all their host by the breath ["spirit" in Hebrew & Greek] of his mouth." Instead, this translation of Genesis 1:1-3 can give the impression that God begins creation from a formless and watery earth, rather than from nothing at all.

Granted, such original chaos may well have been the imaginative picture that the earliest Israelite listeners, who were probably aware of pagan myths of creation, visualized upon hearing this story in Hebrew. Because this NAB translation appears in Catholic liturgical texts, however, both today's listening faithful and also preachers are presented with an imaginative picture that is ironically closer to that visualized by original primitive Hebrew listeners than to the picture presumed for millennia by most generations of Jewish and Christian believers.

This primitivistic reading ignores the entire history of Catholic theological interpretation of Genesis 1:1, including that with which the Gospel of John begins. (See the helpful discussion of four major contemporary interpretations of the first verses of Genesis in Gordon J. Wenham, *Genesis 1-15* [Waco, TX: Word Books, 1987], pp. 11–15.) Instead, our theological reading of Scripture, starting from the beginning of Genesis, will use the classical Revised Standard Version (RSV). When necessary, it will be checked against the traditional Masoretic Hebrew text, its Septuagint Greek translation, and the Vulgate Latin translation. These traditional Hebrew, Greek, and Latin versions and the traditional RSV translation for English speakers have provided the biblical readings on which most Jewish and Christian theology has been based from ancient to modern times.

4. See James L. Kugel, *The Bible as It Was* (Cambridge, MA: The Belknap Press of Harvard University Press, 1997), "The 'Beginning' Did It," pp. 55–57, for samples of very early Jewish and Christian reinterpretation of "In the beginning." Cf. Robert Louis Wilken, *The Spirit of Early Christian Thought: Seeking the Face of God* (New Haven: Yale University Press, 2003), pp. 140–43, on the two meanings of *archē* in Genesis 1:1 as "beginning" and "principle." Wilken emphasizes how the Genesis creation account differs from Greek notions of a demiurge (a minor god) working on shapeless matter, and how it portrays creation as having a purpose, not as a result of chance (pp. 141–42).

5. E.g., aspects of the "six days" of creation in Genesis 1 are described poetically in Psalm 104:2, "who coverest thyself with light as with a garment, who hast stretched out the heavens like a tent," and 104:5-6, "Thou didst set the earth on its foundations, so that it should never be shaken. Thou didst cover it with the deep as with a garment; the waters stood above the mountains." God's providence for his creatures on earth is an intrinsic aspect of the biblical sense of creation, as in Psalm 104:14-15, "Thou dost cause the grass to grow for the cattle, and plants for man to cultivate, that he may bring forth food from the earth, and wine to gladden the heart of man, oil to make his face shine, and bread to strengthen man's heart."

6. Cf. J. M. Casciaro and J. M. Monteforte, *God, the World and Man in the Message of the Bible* (original: *Dios, el Mundo y el Hombre en el Mensaje de la Biblia*, 1992; trans. Michael Adams and James Gavigan; Dublin: Four Courts Press Ltd., 1996), p. 39.

7. Cf. Pope John Paul II, *The Theology of the Body: Human Love in the Divine Plan* (Boston: Pauline Books & Media, 1997). Michael Waldstein's new and more consistent translation with introduction, *Man and Woman He Created Them: A Theology of the Body*, was published by Pauline Books & Media in 2006. See also the helpful commentary by Christopher West, *Theology of the Body Explained: A Commentary on John Paul II's "Gospel of the Body"* (Boston: Pauline Books & Media, 2003).

8. Cf. Wilken, *Early Christian Thought*, pp. 150–51, regarding the patristic claim that the greatness of man is related to being in the image of God the Creator.

CHAPTER 6

READING NEW TESTAMENT PASSAGES THEOLOGICALLY

Christians have generally found it less problematic to read the New Testament theologically than the Old Testament. There are fewer passages in the New Testament than in the Old that are difficult for Christians to understand, that seem to exhibit problematic morality or doctrine, or that seem to have little evident theological significance. As we did with the Old Testament in the last chapter, when reading the New Testament theologically, we will depart from common academic approaches that limit interpretation to only those senses that were available to a reconstructed "original" first-century audience. Instead, following the examples of Sts. Irenaeus and Athanasius, we will read the New Testament in light of the complete salvation narrative of the Bible and the broader context of the teachings of the church, considering their expanded meanings in the complete biblical canon and in later reflection by the church.

To continue the "story," so to speak, that we began in the last chapter, let us begin our illustration of theological reading of New Testament passages as contemporary Christians with some passages from Paul that particularly relate to the dynamics narrated in Genesis 1–3. After the Pauline examples, we will read John 19–20, on Jesus' passion and resurrection, to illustrate the effects of sin and the painful suffering and consequent vindication of the incarnate Son of God (and "Servant" of Isaiah

52–53). Finally, we will look briefly at how the last book in the canon of Scripture, Revelation (or the Apocalypse), describes the turning point of cosmic and human history from the heavenly perspective of God's judgment on evil: the expulsion of Satan from heaven by Michael and his angels as the result of the death and resurrection of the Messiah, and the consequent persecution and temptation of the resultant church by Satan and his worldly agents (the two beasts).

Reading Paul's Letters on the First and Second Adam as Christians Today

Philippians 2: Jesus Compensates for Adam's Sin

In his letters, St. Paul seems to have presumed the same overarching biblical narrative of creation, sin, fall, and salvation that many church fathers later came to use regularly for interpreting the Old Testament. In his Letter to the Philippians, Paul appeals to his Christian followers to imitate the attitude of Jesus, by which we have all been reconciled to God. He implicitly contrasts Jesus' attitude with their temptations to think and act like Adam, who had tried to grasp at "being as God" according to the temptation in Genesis 3:5.[1] Christ's self-sacrificing mindset is the antidote for Adam's self-serving mindset, which had caused humans to become estranged from God. Adam's disobedient self-promotion is comparable to the competition and self-promotion against which Paul is warning his readers. Because the passage itself embodies core elements of the overarching biblical narrative of sin and salvation, its relationships to that narrative are almost self-explanatory.

Paul begins Philippians 2:5-11 by exhorting the Philippians,

"Have this mind among yourselves, which is yours in Christ Jesus, who, *though he was in the form of God, did not count equality with God a thing to be grasped, but emptied himself, taking the form of a servant, being born in the likeness of men*" (Philippians 2:5-7, emphasis added). Adam was created in the image of God in Genesis 1. God's Son, Jesus, existed in the form of God. But unlike Adam, who existed in God's image but wanted more—to actually be equal to God—the Son already existed in a form that was equal to God. In further contrast to Adam, the Son did not cling to his equality with God, whereas Adam succumbed to the temptation of the serpent: "You will be like God, knowing good and evil" (Genesis 3:5). Adam grasped at attaining equality with God by disobeying God's command not to eat of the fruit of the knowledge of good and evil.

In contrast to Adam's attempt at self-promotion and self-glorification, God's Son agreed within the Trinity to become man in order to intervene and save human beings, who were heading toward destruction. The Son emptied himself in the incarnation, by which he "became flesh and dwelt among us" (John 1:14). Incarnate (which is Latin for "enfleshed") as man, the Son had now emptied himself of his divine prerogatives to take on himself the form and existence of the creature man (Philippians 2:7). He lowered himself to the human condition, which included a stringent obligation to obey his Creator, an obligation that could be interpreted and experienced as a condition of "slavery." (The irony of the Son's new condition of being under obligation to man's Creator is increased by the fact that God the Son was himself responsible for man's creation, for "all things [including man] were made through him," John 1:3.)

But what the Son did was more than merely a master's assuming the existential condition of a human slave who was obliged to obey the master who had made him. As man, Jesus freely chose with his human will to become obedient to God's will in an obedience that he knew would lead to his death, even to an agonizing Roman crucifixion. "And being found in human form he humbled himself and became obedient unto death, even death on a cross" (Philippians 2:8). With his human will, the incarnate Son removed the alienation between man and God caused by Adam's willfully disobedient human choices.

The obedience of the incarnate Son of God, even unto his surrendering to death, reversed the disobedience of Adam with its consequence of death. Adam's efforts to grasp at equality to God in knowledge (immortality may also have been implicitly presumed) had resulted in the opposite: the fate of death for every human being as punishment for Adam's sinful disobedience to God. The second Adam, the incarnate Jesus, freely chose for himself a death, even death on the cross, which he had neither deserved nor would have had to undergo if he had not already emptied himself to take on the form of a human slave in obedience to God's will and plan for him. And in so doing, he overcame death and redeemed humanity.

Whereas Adam's disobedience had banished him from God's presence and friendship and caused him to lose many of his special privileges as having dominion over material creation, Jesus' obedience led to his resurrection and exaltation and to his receiving the name of "Lord," which was above every other name. (In the Old Testament, "LORD" was the primary name that Israelites used for God.) Now, at the name of the glorified Lord Jesus, every knee shall bow, "and every tongue confess that *Jesus Christ is Lord*, to the glory of God the Father" (Philippians 2:11, emphasis added). The exaltation of the servant (slave) of the Lord in Isaiah is now seen in hindsight to be a hitherto unimaginable exaltation above every creature in the cosmos, all of whom would call Jesus "*Lord*, to the glory of God the Father."

By his obedience, Jesus has now attained the name above every name, "Lord," but his name does not compete in glory with the name of his Father. Reading this passage theologically as we learned from Athanasius, we realize that because of the unity of Father and Son, in that they share the same being and essence (*homoousios*), glory given to the Lord Jesus is glory given to God the Father. Paul's reference to all creatures' calling Jesus "Lord, to the glory of God the Father," makes even more sense when read theologically with reference to the one God existing as the Trinity of co-equal Father, Son, and Holy Spirit.

Romans 5 & 1 Corinthians 15: Further Contrasting Jesus and Adam

We can supplement this reading from Philippians with brief references to two related Pauline passages that contrast Adam with Jesus—Romans 5 and 1 Corinthians 15. As the church fathers reflected on its implications, Romans 5 became a major inspiration for the Catholic doctrine of original sin. The RSV follows the original Greek closely in translating Paul's further thought (after he said that sin came into the world through Adam and death through sin) as follows: "and so death spread to all men *because* all men sinned" (Romans 5:12, emphasis added). The Latin translation that influenced St. Augustine and much subsequent Western Catholic theology on original sin, however, said that death spread to all men "*in whom*" [in Adam] all sinned.

In Romans 5:15, Paul again directly links death to Adam's

sin. "But the free gift is not like the trespass. For *if many died through one man's trespass*, much more have the grace of God and the *free gift in the grace of that one man Jesus Christ* abounded for many" (Romans 5:15, emphasis added). As death came to all men through Adam, so God's free gift of grace comes to all men through Jesus, the second Adam. Paul lays out the implications of this contrast between the first and second Adam and their effects on subsequent human condemnation and death or justification:

> And the free gift is not like the effect of that one man's sin. For the judgment following one trespass brought condemnation, but the free gift following many trespasses brings justification. If, because of one man's trespass, death reigned through that one man, much more will those who receive the abundance of grace and the free gift of righteousness reign in life through the one man Jesus Christ.
>
> Then as one man's trespass led to condemnation for all men, so one man's act of righteousness leads to acquittal and life for all men. For as by one man's disobedience many were made sinners, so by one man's obedience many will be made righteous. (Romans 5:16-19)

Paul here underscores how much greater is the gift won through Christ than the condemnation that followed the sin of Adam. God's judgment on Adam's one sin had brought condemnation, but the free gift won by the second Adam, despite countless human sins, brings justification. Because of Adam's one sin, death has reigned through Adam, but even more will all who are justified by Christ, the new Adam, reign in life through him.

Adam's sin led to condemnation for the whole human race. Jesus' act of righteousness (especially his self-sacrificing death on the cross) brings acquittal from condemnation and the prospect of life for all humans. Adam's disobedience made many people sinners, whereas the second Adam's obedience will make many people righteous. All throughout this passage, Paul is reflecting on Genesis 3 in light of the good news about Jesus.

Paul ends his reflection with this conclusion that contrasts death through Adam with eternal life through the second Adam: "So that, as sin reigned in death, grace also might reign through righteousness to eternal life through Jesus Christ our Lord" (Romans 5:21). Sin had had dominion over man through death and the human fear of death (cf. Hebrews 2:14-15).[2] Now, through the second Adam, Christ, grace brings righteousness, overcomes death, and has dominion through eternal life.

1 Corinthians 15:20-28 also contrasts Christ, the second Adam who brings resurrection, with the first Adam, who had brought death. As St. Paul reflects on the end of time, he sees Christ reversing the destructive effects related to Adam. He contrasts the death that came through Adam with the resurrection from the dead that comes from Christ. "For as in Adam all die, so also in Christ shall all be made alive" (15:22). Christ has already risen as a kind of "first fruit" or initial occurrence of human resurrection from death. Those who belong to Christ will also be made alive "at his coming" (15:23). "Then comes the end, when he delivers the kingdom to God the Father after destroying every rule and every authority and power" (15:24).

God's original plan of creation was that Adam and the human race should "have dominion" over all of material creation (Genesis 1:26-28). After Adam's disobedience to his Creator God, he effectively lost much of his dominion. Instead of plants' yielding to Adam fruit that he could effortlessly pick and eat, they now yielded to him "thorns and thistles" (Genesis 3:18). Henceforth, Adam could obtain food from the earth and its plants only after much labor and the "sweat of his face" (3:17-19). Meanwhile, many of the later Old Testament books as well as the New Testament regarded Satan as having usurped the weakened dominion of humans over the world. Satan was in control of so much of it that Jesus could refer to him as ruler of this world ("Now is the judgment of this world, now shall the ruler of this world be cast out," John 12:31).

However, at the end of the world, Christ will return to conquer Satan and all evil spirits, and ultimately conquer death (see 1 Corinthians 15:26). "When all things are subjected to him, then the Son himself will also be subjected to him who put all things under him, that God may be everything to every one" (15:28). All creatures will be subjected to the Son, who is ultimately subjected to the Father within the Trinity. In the final triumph of the glorified Son of God and second Adam, the human race will regain from the usurper Satan the dominion over creation that God in Genesis had intended for humans when creating them.

The original meanings of these Pauline passages are already quite theological. Reading them, however, with explicit reference to the overall biblical story of salvation, however, as the church fathers habitually did, makes their implications in the broader theological context more explicit. Such openly explicit theological reading also relates them more immediately to the lives of contemporary Christian readers.

Reading the Passion and Resurrection Narratives as Christians Today

The passion and resurrection narratives in John 19–20 can provide further examples of reading New Testament passages theologically in the context of the overall biblical narrative of salvation. Following the patterns demonstrated by Sts. Irenaeus and Athanasius, it is possible to emphasize the theological message of these accounts by explicitly situating them within this biblical salvation narrative. Contextualizing these accounts in this way is made easier by the fact that the gospel author has already presented them against the backdrop of the Old Testament story of creation, the fall, and salvation.

Jesus' Identity and Irony

After Pilate had Jesus scourged and the soldiers had further mocked him with a crown of thorns and purple robe as "King of the Jews," Pilate presented Jesus to the people with the statement, "Behold *the man*" (Greek *anthrōpos* [John 19:5], the generic term for the first human, Adam). The first man had tried to share God's divine prerogatives and, consequently, had lost much of the dominion God had granted him. Now Jesus, as "the man" atones for Adam's grasping after divine power by suffering mockery and rejection under the title "King of the Jews," whose crucifixion his own compatriots ironically demand.

John's gospel immediately reminds readers of the underlying mystery about the identity of Jesus, "the man" who is standing before Pilate and the people. John quotes the charge of the Jewish leaders, "We have a law, and by that law he ought to die, because *he has made himself the Son of God*" (John 19:7). This allegation that Jesus had claimed divinity disturbs Pilate and prompts him to question *where Jesus is from*. The mystery of Jesus' origins has been a principal theme running throughout John's gospel. Throughout the gospel, some people are ignorant of Jesus' origins. Others, like Nicodemus, misunderstand references about where Jesus comes from (in John 3).

The groundwork for this Johannine theme of the mystery of Jesus' origins has been laid by the explicit revelation made in the prologue of John 1. Before the narrative of Jesus' ministry begins, the narrator explains that he pre-existed creation as Word and Son of God, that everything was created through him, that he "became flesh and dwelt among us," but that when he came among his own, they rejected him. The prologue concludes with this explanation: "No one has ever seen God; the only Son, who is in the bosom of the Father, he has made him known" (John 1:18). Jesus would later confirm this claim when he explained to Philip in his last supper discourse, "*He who has seen me has seen the Father*; how can you say, 'Show us the Father'?" (14:9, emphasis added).

After Pilate receives no response from Jesus, he presents him again to the people: "*Behold your King!*" (see John 19:14). This, in turn, elicits from the crowd the ironic declaration that they have no king but Caesar (see 19:15), a particularly bitter admission in view of the people's deep and longstanding desire for independence from the Romans. This irony is further emphasized by the official charge that Pilate orders to be affixed to Jesus' cross, "*Jesus of Nazareth, the King of the Jews*" and his refusal to nuance it (see 19:19-22).

The theology of John's gospel relies heavily on Johannine irony, in which readers are aware of meaning that is not understood by characters within the narrative. Here the irony regarding Jesus' kingship is emphasized. As a prelude to Jesus' passion, John's gospel had shown him entering Jerusalem on a donkey to acclamations by the crowds as "*King of Israel*" (John 12:12-16, especially v. 13). John emphasizes that this event fulfilled Old Testament prophecy: "'Fear not, daughter of Zion; behold, *your king is coming*, sitting on an ass's colt!' [Zechariah 9:9]. His disciples did not understand this at first; but when Jesus was glorified, then they remembered that this had been written of him and had been done to him" (John 12:15-16). Then, later that same week, the crowd rejects Jesus as king before Pilate and even declares, "We have no king but Caesar" (19:15). Whereas Jesus' countrymen reject him as king, Pilate contemptuously insists on his kingship in his formal charges.

The irony of the contrast between Jesus' entry into Jerusalem as "King of Israel" and his later rejection by the crowds as "King of the Jews" emphasizes the unanticipated way in which Jesus fulfills Old Testament expectations regarding a savior king. Jesus is clearly not a king in the political meaning of the acclamations by the crowds during his entry into Jerusalem. In that sense, Jesus is in fact no rival to Caesar, as Pilate's statements make clear. Yet, in another sense, Jesus is indeed the "King of Israel" who is expected in the Old Testament (as in Zechariah 9:9). Pilate's refusal to change the inscription he had placed on Jesus' cross ironically confirms this title.

Although the human actors (Pilate and the hostile crowds) do not realize the truth, John presents Jesus as "the man" (the second Adam) who will ironically be "glorified" by being raised up on the cross as "King of the Jews." Thus, he fulfills the prophecy made earlier in the gospel by the high priest

Caiaphas, "You do not understand that it is expedient for you *that one man should die for the people*, and that the whole nation should not perish" (John 11:50). A key aspect of the mystery that this gospel proclaims is that the "one man" who is to die for the people is the Son of God who "became flesh" (i.e., became incarnate, 1:14).

The statement by Caiaphas contains a double irony. He had rendered his pronouncement as a political expedient to avoid the wrath of Rome. However, both Christian author and Christian readers understand Caiaphas' meaning as ironically referring to the atonement that "one man" (the incarnate Son of God who is undoing the harm done by Adam, the original man) is to make by dying for the people. John portrays these scenes in the context of the overall biblical narrative of salvation, in which the Son of God has become incarnate to die for the sins of Adam and all humans (as "Lamb of God" John 1:29, 36), in order to undo human disobedience by his obedience as human to his Father.

Jesus Hands Over His Mother and His Spirit to the Church

John's account of Jesus' death looks back to fulfillment of Old Testament prophecy and forward to empowering and equipping the future church of his disciples. He is the only Evangelist to report how Jesus entrusts his mother to his beloved disciple before his death. Symbolic aspects of this account are accentuated by Jesus' unusual use of titles and addresses. The narrator never names Mary, but refers to her simply as "his [Jesus'] mother," as he had also previously called her in his only other account concerning Mary, the wedding at Cana.

Not only does the narrator fail to name Mary either here or at Cana, but neither does Jesus address Mary in either account as readers might expect—as "Mother." Rather, he addresses her as "Woman." The emphasis on *woman* again recalls the first woman, Eve, and her role in humanity's fall from intimacy with God. Both at Cana and at the cross, John's gospel implies a contrast between the role of the first woman and mother of the human race in the fall of humans by inducing Adam to sin, and the role of this *woman* and mother of reborn humans in their redemption by influencing the beginning of the saving "signs" of the second Adam, Jesus.

Jesus' declaration "Woman, behold, your son," as well as his reciprocal "Behold, your mother," pronounce the adoption of his beloved disciple by his mother as her own son. By addressing Mary as *woman* rather than as *mother,* Jesus emphasizes Mary's role as the woman of the new creation. Whereas the first woman, Eve, was the "mother of all living" (Genesis 3:20), in the new creation that Jesus is bringing about, the woman Mary, as a new Eve, is to be mother of all his beloved disciples who are *reborn* into Jesus' eternal life.

Avoidance of the beloved disciple's name also emphasizes the symbolic aspects of his role in the narrative. Ideally, every Christian follower of Jesus would want to be considered Jesus' "beloved disciple." Therefore, in this account, the beloved disciple can easily symbolize the church made up of Jesus' followers. When Jesus asks his mother as woman to be mother of his beloved disciple, this can have the added symbolic significance of Mary's becoming mother of the church of Jesus' followers. The title of Mary as mother of the church was recently confirmed by Vatican II's *Lumen Gentium* and reemphasized by Pope Paul VI as quoted in the *Catechism* § 975: "We believe that the *Holy Mother of God, the new Eve, Mother of the Church*, continues in heaven to exercise her maternal role on behalf of the members of Christ" (Paul VI, *Credo of the People of God* § 15, with emphasis added).

Jesus' final words on the cross, "It is finished," have more than one level of meaning, as do many statements in John's gospel. The Gospel of John had repeatedly insisted that the sabbath from God's creative activity that Genesis 1 announced had not yet, in fact, been fully realized. God's creative work and actions were continuing, particularly in the work and actions of the saving ministry of his Son, Jesus, in the gospel. Recall especially John 5:16-18:

> And this was why the Jews persecuted Jesus, because he did this on the sabbath. But Jesus answered them, "*My Father is working still, and I am working.*" This was why the Jews sought all the more to kill him, because he not only broke the sabbath but also called God his Father, making himself equal with God. (emphasis added)

That is, for John's gospel, God's work of creation was not, in fact, fully completed with the Genesis declaration of God's sabbath on the seventh day. In John's gospel, God is continuing (especially through his incarnate Son, Jesus) to work toward a new creation. This creative activity of Father and Son will only finally be "finished" when Jesus dies on the cross and hands over his Holy Spirit to the church, represented by the mother and beloved disciple standing at the foot of his cross.

Jesus' final statement, "It is finished" (John 19:30), indicates that the work the Father had given him to do in his incarnate ministry has now been completed. In addition, the statement implies that the biblical prophecies about Jesus have been fulfilled.

The second part of verse 30, the description of Jesus' actual death, also has at least two levels of meaning. The RSV version, "and he bowed his head and gave up his spirit," focuses primarily on Jesus death, using terms regularly used for dying, such as "giving up one's spirit," or, in older terminology, "giving up the ghost." The Greek original, however, clearly has a double meaning that does not appear clearly in the RSV translation.

The Greek term *paredōken,* which the RSV translates "and gave up his spirit," also signifies "handing over" or "passing on" [e.g., an office, as in ordination], which also refers to tradition. The Greek clearly implies a second meaning beyond a mere description of Jesus' last breath. It can also be understood to say "and he handed over his Spirit" in the sense that at his death Jesus handed over and passed on the Holy Spirit to his mother and beloved disciple as representatives of his future church.

The incidents that follow Jesus' death receive extraordinary emphasis in John's gospel as climactic evidence of and witness to the meaning of his death. In contrast to the two criminals with him, Jesus was already dead and, therefore, did not have his legs broken. John interprets this as fulfilling the biblical Passover regulations (also understood as prophecy)—"Not a bone of him shall be broken" (John 19:36, alluding to Exodus 12:46, "In one house shall it [the Passover lamb] be eaten; you shall not carry forth any of the flesh outside the house; *and you shall not break a bone of it.*")[3] Very early in the gospel, John the Baptist had given witness to Jesus by announcing, "Behold, the Lamb of God, who takes away the sin of the world!" (John 1:29; see also 1:36). This scene in John's gospel demonstrates how "the Lamb of God" by his death (a death that followed the prescriptions for slaughtering the Passover lamb) brings about the salvation of God's people, as had the deaths of the original Passover lambs during the exodus.

Even more emphasis falls on the beloved disciple's explicit witness to how the dead Jesus' side was pierced and how *blood and water came out* (see John 19:34-35). Insistence on the veracity of this witness is a clear signal of how pivotal this event is regarded for the interpretation of Jesus' death: "He who saw it has borne witness—his testimony is true, and he knows that he tells the truth—that you also may believe" (19:35). Almost all commentators and church fathers see the outpouring of blood and water as deeply symbolic. Many compare this flow of blood and water from the side of the dead Jesus to Adam's spouse Eve's being taken from Adam's side as he slept in Genesis 2:21-23. Because blood and water frequently symbolize the key sacraments of Eucharist and baptism, together they can symbolize the birth of the church (often referred to as the spouse of Christ) from his side after his death.

At the end of John 21 (the "second ending" of the gospel), the following claim is made regarding the beloved disciple: "This is the disciple who is bearing witness to these things, and who has written these things; and we know that his testimony is true" (John 21:24). That final claim reinforces the statement about the veracity of witness in John 19:35, "He who saw it has borne witness—his testimony is true, and he knows that he tells the truth—that you also may believe." The gospel goes out of its way to emphasize, even with repetition, that its account is based on the true witness of the beloved disciple, who was an eyewitness of Jesus' death (and later of his resurrection). The beloved disciple who is responsible for the witness of this fourth gospel has borne witness to the flow of blood and water (and thus to the birth of the church that it symbolizes) from the body of the dead Jesus.

John 20: Jesus' Resurrection and Our Need to Believe

When Jesus first appeared to the apostles following his resurrection, Thomas had not been present, and so he refused to believe the good news, the witness of the others to the gospel, "We have seen the Lord" (John 20:25a). "Unless I see in his hands the print of the nails, and place my finger in the mark of the nails, and place my hand in his side," Thomas replied, "*I will not believe*" (20:25b).

When Jesus reappeared the following Sunday, he rebuked Thomas for his refusal to believe. "Put your finger here, and see my hands; and put out your hand, and place it in my side; *do not be faithless, but believing*" (John 20:27). Even though Thomas responded with the clearest and strongest declaration of the divinity of Jesus in John's entire gospel, Jesus drew for Thomas an important lesson that applies to all future Christian believers. In response to Thomas' statement of faith, "My Lord and my God!" (20:28), Jesus answered, "*Have you believed because you have seen me? Blessed are those who have not seen and yet believe*" (20:29).

This pronouncement by the risen Jesus summarizes one of the gospel's main emphases, the critical necessity of believing the good news about Jesus. For all Christians who live after Jesus' return to the Father and who, therefore, cannot see him in the flesh, faith will depend on heeding the church's message that we are saved through the death and resurrection of Jesus. Faith will demand that all later Christians (including ourselves many centuries later) believe the witness of those original disciples of Jesus, which is written in this gospel: "And the Word became flesh and *dwelt among us*, full of grace and truth; *we have beheld his glory*, glory as of the only Son from the Father" (John 1:14, emphasis added).

Chapter twenty ends with a declaration of the purpose of writing the gospel.[4] "Now Jesus did many other signs in the presence of the disciples, which are not written in this book; but *these are written that you may believe that Jesus is the Christ, the Son of God, and that believing you may have life in his name*" (John 20:30-31, emphasis added). The signs that are recounted in this gospel are provided as helps for readers to have faith that Jesus is the Son of God and the Christ, or Messiah, whom the Old Testament has been expecting. According to the gospel, this belief in Jesus' identity as God and man who fulfills the Old Testament prophetic expectations is the foundational prerequisite for sharing in the eternal life that the Son of God came to give.

Reading Revelation—the Bible's "Last Word"—as Christians Today

Our last example of theological reading of Scripture will be a climactic turning point in the final book of the biblical canon, Revelation, which portrays the end of the world and the final goal and consummation of God's creation, with which our Old Testament examples began. The sample is Revelation 11:15–13:18, which depicts the fulfillment of God's kingdom after the seventh and final trumpet is blown. Revelation 11:15-19 begins this section by celebrating how God's kingdom has finally come and judgment has finally been passed, so that the long-suffering innocent on earth can now receive reward and relief from oppression by their oppressors.

"Then the seventh angel blew his trumpet, and there were loud voices in heaven, saying, '*The kingdom of the world has become the kingdom of our Lord and of his Christ, and he shall reign for ever and ever*'" (Revelation 11:15, emphasis added). Finally, after the seventh trumpet, heaven could celebrate that at the end of time, the Lord God and his Messiah have at last restored God's kingdom on earth. God's kingdom had been compromised almost at the very beginning of time after Adam forfeited most of the dominion that God had delegated to him as his image and representative. Finally, at the end of time, Satan and all his forces of oppression (who during human history had usurped most of the dominion that God had delegated to Adam and humanity at creation) have been ousted from power.

The song of the twenty-four elders in heaven (probably representing the twelve tribes of God's Old Testament people and the twelve apostles of the church) celebrates that God has finally established his power and reign over the earth. He has conquered and destroyed all nations and evil forces, pronounced his final judgment over the earth, and given relief to those who have remained faithful to him.

> We give thanks to thee, Lord God Almighty,
>   who art and who wast,
>   that thou hast taken thy great power and begun to reign.
> The nations raged, but *thy wrath came*,
>   and *the time for the dead to be judged*,
>   for *rewarding thy servants*, the prophets and saints,

and those who fear thy name, both small and great,
and for *destroying the destroyers of the earth.*
(Revelation 11:17-18, emphasis added)

Revelation here emphasizes a dogmatic truth about the meaning of human life and what happens after death, which has become distressingly neglected the last few generations. Today many high school and university students seem quite ignorant of any idea about what, if anything, might happen to them after their deaths. Others refuse to consider what awaits them at and after death, dismissing the question as nonsense. What is evidently lacking from the catechesis or training in Catholicism of many members of our younger generations is any sense of what has traditionally been called "the four last things"—death, judgment, heaven, and hell.

This passage from Revelation recalls the fact that there will be a judgment for every human being at the end. Although the end to which Revelation here refers is primarily the end of human history, logically the notion of *end* can also be extended to the end of each individual's bodily life on earth. We need to recall that all of us will face "the time for the dead to be judged." That judgment will result either in "rewarding thy [God's] servants," or in punishing those who do harm and evil on earth. Recalling that none of us who have been created by God can escape judgment by our Creator for how we live our lives on earth would go a long way toward restoring and strengthening among both young and old a personal sense of morality and a moral urgency about God's commandments.

This song of praise also helps explain the meaning and function of the biblical notion of God's "wrath," which many people find disturbing. God's wrath is a metaphor to describe God's just reaction to evil and to the harm and oppression that evildoers inflict on the innocent. "Wrath" is a term taken from human emotions and applied here, however inadequately, to God. The context in Revelation 11:18 applies the term "wrath" to judgment by God that both rewards the holy and destroys "the destroyers of the earth."

Within the overall context of God's judgment of all humans' behavior, the emphasis in the term "wrath" is on condemnation of evil. Even wrath, however, is ultimately inspired by God's love. Because God loves sinners and desires them to return his love, it is a natural human comparison to portray God as displeased when sinners refuse his love. The context here in Revelation relates God's wrath even more explicitly, however, to God's love for the innocent victims of evil actions. Just as a father, out of love of his child, becomes angry with an assailant that he sees attacking the child, so, too, God, out of love for his oppressed human children, naturally feels "wrath" for their oppressors.

When worldly powers seem under the control of primarily evil forces, only a greater power—that of God—can wrest that control from oppressors and restore God's own just and peaceful order and rule over the earth. Only in this way will the innocent be freed from oppression by evil persons or institutions. Ultimately, Revelation expects this definitive restoration of God's kingdom over the earth only after God's last judgment and final destruction of evil.

Signs and Portents in Heaven: The Woman and the Dragon

After this climactic song of praise that God's kingdom had finally begun on earth, the prophet John reports seeing a vision in heaven of God's heavenly temple (which has replaced the lost earthly temple). Now that the earthly temple has been destroyed and the Ark of the Covenant lost, the prophet sees the Ark of the Covenant in God's temple in heaven along with lightning, thunder, earthquake, and hail (which might be considered the "apocalyptic stage props" routinely mentioned in visions of the end times). This vision is the backdrop for the appearance of the momentous double portent of the woman and the dragon (see Revelation 12).

The woman in heaven is described in cosmic terms as "clothed with the sun, with the moon under her feet, and on her head a crown of twelve stars" (Revelation 12:1).[5] Genesis 37:9-10 had used the same imagery in Joseph's dream for the twelve sons (and, therefore, tribes) of Israel: "Behold, I have dreamed another dream; and behold, the sun, the moon, and eleven stars were bowing down to me." Joseph's father, Israel, had rebuked him, "What is this dream that you have dreamed? Shall I and your mother and your brothers indeed come to bow ourselves to the ground before you?" Against this background, the woman crowned with the twelve stars seems to refer to Israel with its twelve tribes, from which would come the Messiah.

The heavenly woman cried out in pangs of birth (Revelation 12:2) and "she brought forth a male child, one who is to rule all the nations with a rod of iron, but her child was caught up to God and to his throne" (12:5). The imagery makes clear that the woman's son is the Messiah who would rule all nations. Although many readers, including many church fathers, presumed that this vision of birth refers to the birth of Jesus from Mary, the context suggests that this vision refers primarily not to the Messiah's birth but rather to his death and resurrection.

In apocalyptic writings about the end times, birth pangs are a common image for the sufferings involved in the birth of a new age (which the Jewish rabbis called the "world to come"). In this passage, birth pangs describe well the suffering involved in the transition to the new age of salvation, with its new covenant, that occurred as Israel gave birth to the rule of the Messiah through the death and resurrection of Jesus. The vision of the painful birth at which the dragon is waiting and expecting to devour the Messiah implies that Satan was confident that he was about to be victorious over Jesus at the occasion of his death on the cross. "And the dragon stood before the woman who was about to bear a child, that he might devour her child when she brought it forth" (Revelation 12:4). The moment that the "male child . . . who is to rule all the nations with a rod of iron" came forth from Israel, however, "her child was caught up to God and to his throne" (Revelation 12:5).

The imagery fits well the circumstances of Israel as the woman giving birth to the victorious rule of the Messiah, which was inaugurated through Jesus' death, resurrection, and ascension to God's throne. By rising after death, the Messiah cheated the expectations of victory that Satan had when Jesus died on the cross. Just when Satan thought he had conquered the dead Jesus, the death that he had instigated ironically opened the way in God's mysterious wisdom for Jesus to be exalted as "Lord of glory." Thinking to quash any possible messianic future for Jesus by having him crucified, Satan ironically made possible his enthronement as Lord of glory at the Father's right hand.

This image of Satan's being tricked and cheated of his expectations of victory reminds me of St. Paul's statement in his First Letter to the Corinthians:

> Yet among the mature we do impart wisdom, although it is not a wisdom of this age or of *the rulers of this age*, who are doomed to pass away. But we impart a secret and hidden wisdom of God, which God decreed before the ages for our glorification. *None of the rulers of this age understood this; for if they had, they would not have crucified the Lord of glory.* (1 Corinthians 2:6-8, emphasis added)

In Paul's First Letter to the Corinthians, "rulers of this age" refers not only to the human rulers who had Jesus put to death, but also to Satan and his evil spirits, who inspired their earthly minions to that decision. The Pauline image of demonic "rulers of this age" working through human rulers and institutions is parallel to the image in Revelation of the dragon, Satan, achieving his ends through the beast from the sea, Rome.

In Revelation 12, the dragon itself is described with similar symbolism as that used for beasts that had represented evil powers in earlier apocalyptic books of the Bible, like Daniel. Revelation explicitly identifies the dragon with the serpent of Genesis and with Satan (see Revelation 12:9 and 20:2).

This extended vision has two levels. On one level, the dragon was waiting on earth to devour the Messiah. On the other level, a battle took place in heaven. The battle in heaven in which Satan and his evil angels are expelled is the heavenly counterpart and result of the earthly death and resurrection of the Messiah, Jesus. John sees in his vision a battle in heaven in which Michael and his angels defeat Satan and his angels and cast them out of heaven onto earth. This occasions a song of triumph in heaven, which expresses the heart of Revelation's message of salvation:

> Now the salvation and the power and the kingdom of our God and the authority of his Christ have come, for the accuser of our brethren has been thrown down, who accuses them day and night before our God. And they have conquered him by the blood of the Lamb and by the word of their testimony, for they loved not their lives even unto death. Rejoice then, O heaven and you that dwell therein! But woe to you, O earth and sea, for the devil has come down to you in great wrath, because he knows that his time is short! (Revelation 12:10-12)

The song attributes this victory over Satan to "the blood of the Lamb" (Jesus), but also to "the word of their testimony, for they loved not their lives even unto death." In some way that is not explained, the victory over Satan that was primarily won by the death of Jesus was also confirmed by the witness even unto death of the Christian martyrs. After Jesus' death and resurrection, Satan, the prosecuting attorney who has been accusing guilty humans before God's throne of judgment, has finally been expelled from heaven.

After their own death, therefore, when humans arrive before God's throne for judgment, the lack of the prosecuting attorney (Satan) symbolizes that they will not be prosecuted as they deserve. Even though humans are guilty before God's judgment throne, they are not punished with hell, because their guilt has been forgiven through the death and resurrection of Jesus. In the imaginative form of a vision, this imagery cannot fully be equated with more rationally expressed church doctrine. Still, it expresses the truth that although all humans are sinners who formerly lived in dread of the accusations by the prosecuting attorney, Satan, they can now hope to obtain forgiveness because of Jesus' death and resurrection. One contemporary theological expression for this is that we are "saved by grace" (won for us by Jesus), not by our own righteousness or works.

Satan's expulsion from heaven gives hope that we can be saved after our deaths, when we appear before God's heavenly throne of judgment. This is the "good news" of the vision, which is expressed in the rejoicing in heaven over Satan's removal. The "bad news" of this vision, however, is the devil's wrath at his loss of being able to accuse humans before heaven's judgment throne.

His wrath is aggravated because of the brief window of opportunity left to him to afflict those still alive on earth. "Rejoice then, O heaven and you that dwell therein! But woe to you, O earth and sea, for the devil has come down to you in great wrath, because he knows that his time is short!" (Revelation 12:12). When bullies lose to someone stronger than they, they often pick on someone weaker. Satan's defeat by Jesus' death and resurrection leads him to persecute the woman and her other children. "Then the dragon was angry with the woman, and went off to make war on the rest of her offspring, on those who keep the commandments of God and bear testimony to Jesus" (Revelation 12:17).

Identification of the woman's other offspring as "those who keep the commandments of God *and bear testimony to Jesus*" makes clear that the woman's other offspring are Christians. This, in turn, implies that the woman is now identified with (mother) church. Earlier, the vision had identified the woman with Israel's giving birth to the Messiah, but now the identification of the woman shifts to the church.

Such transition of meanings in visions is not unusual. Psychologists treat the subconscious dynamics of visions and dreams as similar (for both of them feature imaginative images that are not consciously controlled by the visionary or dreamer). All of us can remember dreams in which images in the dream change identities or meaning part way through the dream. For better or for worse, in the dream we unexpectedly find ourselves in a changed situation or with someone new.

The change in meaning of this image of the woman—from the Old Testament woman, Israel, giving birth to the Messiah, to the New Testament woman, the church, having other children (Christians)—is a relatively simple one and not unexpected for dreams or visions. In addition, Catholic readers are aware of Mary's being made mother of the beloved disciple (and, thus, of the church) at the foot of the cross in John 19. Hence, a further allusion to Mary within this symbol of the woman seems a natural theological extension of the original understanding of the woman as first, God's Old Testament people, and second, his New Testament people, the church.

The Dragon Attacks the Woman and Her Offspring through the Beast

The last verse of Revelation 12 provides a transition from the vision of the dragon to the vision of the beast rising from the sea. "Then the dragon was angry with the woman, and went off to make war on the rest of her offspring, on those who keep the commandments of God and bear testimony to Jesus. *And he stood on the sand of the sea*" (Revelation 12:17). The focus on the dragon in this extended vision ends with the dragon standing on the seashore awaiting the arrival of the beast from the sea. Rather than always attacking the Christian children of the woman personally, Satan the dragon waits for the arrival of the beast, through which much of his war against Christians will be waged.

Revelation 13 begins with the seer reporting a vision of a beast emerging from the sea. "And I saw a beast rising out of the sea, with ten horns and seven heads, with ten diadems upon its horns and a blasphemous name upon its heads" (Revelation 13:1). The beast has the same number of horns and diadems or crowns as the dragon, symbolizing the same power as the dragon. This sharing of diabolic power is made explicit by the statement, "And to it [the beast] the dragon gave his power and his throne and great authority" (13:2).

The beast to which the dragon has delegated his authority over the earth is described with particulars that refer especially to the Roman Empire at the time of writing. The healing of the mortal wound of one of the heads seems to refer to rumors that the persecuting emperor Nero (who had died in ambiguous circumstances) was still alive. This death-resurrection imagery also diabolically mimics the death and resurrection of the Lamb who was slain standing near God's throne (see Revelation 5:6).

In Revelation there is a kind of contest in which the dragon and beast mimic God and the Lamb. The dragon and beast often counterfeit marks and signs worked by God and the Lamb, as well as responses that people give to God and the Lamb. For example, some people worshiped the dragon and Rome (his beast representative) as others worshiped God and the Lamb. The reaction to the beast clearly alluded to the usual reaction to the Roman empire and its overwhelming power at the time of Revelation: "Who can fight against it?" According to Christian sensitivities, Rome also frequently made blasphemous statements, including claims that Roman emperors were divine. Just as in Daniel 7, when the evil Greek emperor had a limited time period in which he got away with his blasphemous actions, so Rome was now enjoying a similar limited period in which its blasphemies were going unchecked:

> Men worshiped the dragon, for he had given his authority to the beast, and they worshiped the beast, saying, "Who is like the beast, and who can fight against it?" And the beast was given a mouth uttering haughty and blasphemous words, and it was allowed to exercise authority for forty-two months. (Revelation 13:4-5)

This beast was also permitted (ultimately by God) to overcome individual Christians. Under Roman persecution, many Christians suffered and died, including Sts. Peter and Paul, who were martyred in Rome under the emperor Nero in the early sixties.

> Also it [the beast] was allowed to make war on the saints and to conquer them. And authority was given it over every tribe and people and tongue and nation, and all who dwell on earth will worship it, every one whose name has not been written before the foundation of the world in the book of life of the Lamb that was slain. (Revelation 13:7-8)

Christian persecution was historically only a minor aspect of the political authority and domination of the Roman Empire, which expanded to most of the known world "over every tribe and people and tongue and nation." Rome's authority was often treated as divine authority, especially in the eastern part of the empire: "All who dwell on earth will worship it." This prophetic vision admits that Rome's power and persecution would result in Christians' being captured or slain. Consequently, "Here is a call for the endurance and faith of the saints" (Revelation 13:10).

Revelation 13:11-18 continues the vision with John's seeing a *second beast* rising out of the earth (a counterpart to the first beast from the sea). The second beast is even more explicitly compared to the Lamb than the first had been. "Then I saw another beast which rose out of the earth; it had two horns like a lamb and it spoke like a dragon" (Revelation 13:11). The second beast was plainly trying to imitate and resemble the Messiah (the Lamb). When it spoke, however, its message gave it away as a false messiah, because its voice was clearly the voice of the demonic dragon. Not only is this second beast pictured as a false messiah by the details with which it is described, but it is also explicitly labeled a false prophet by the narrator. Whereas a prophet is true if he speaks the messages of God, the second beast is a false prophet because he speaks the messages of Satan, the dragon.

The second beast is explicitly a mouthpiece and instrument through which the first beast exercises its authority. "It exercises all the authority of the first beast in its presence, and makes the earth and its inhabitants worship the first beast, whose mortal wound was healed" (Revelation 13:12). Although there is almost a consensus among biblicists that the first beast originally referred to the Roman Empire, there are varying conjectures over the identity of the second beast. Most regard it as some kind of authority structure in the empire, such as a Roman province, local Roman priests or officers, or a provincial bureaucracy.

It seems sufficient simply to mention the main theological point that this vision provides about the beasts. The ultimate cause of rejection and persecution of Christians in this world is Satan (the dragon), but he generally works his mischief and harm through human institutions and persons (such as through the Roman Empire and its authority structure at the time of the writing of Revelation). The second beast works signs to deceive people into believing in the false claims to divine authority made by the first beast. This is described in ways that can symbolize Rome in the first century, but it can also apply to any comparable later political or national structures or ideologies that seize control and make life miserable for Christians, such as the Nazis under Hitler or Communists under Stalin.

The final part of this vision has generated considerable confusion and controversy. The second beast is shown mimicking God's marking of Christians with the seal of the Lamb to indicate that they belong to him. In Revelation 7 one angel had commanded other angels, who had been commissioned to destroy parts of the earth, *first to mark or seal those who serve God so that they will be passed over by the destroying angels.* "Do not harm the earth or the sea or the trees, till we have sealed the servants of our God upon their foreheads" (Revelation 7:3).

This alluded to God's salvation of his people from Egyptian slavery and oppression at the exodus. During the exodus from Egypt, marking the Israelites' doors with the blood of the Passover lamb had signaled to the angel of death to pass over their homes without killing their firstborn (see Exodus 12:7-14). In Revelation 7, the mark of the Lamb on the believers had again spared them from the punishing angel.

Now the second beast is marking everyone with another mark, the mark of the beast, which is required for economic undertakings. The lack of the mark of the beast results in some form of economic persecution for Christians who refuse to be identified with the mark of the beast. "Also it causes all, both small and great, both rich and poor, both free and slave, to be marked on the right hand or the forehead, *so that no one can buy or sell unless he has the mark, that is, the name of the beast* or the number of its name" (Revelation 13:16-17, emphasis added).

In Revelation 7, the first mark had preserved Christians from end-time plagues that angels were about to inflict on evildoers. The mark of the beast is a mocking reversal of the mark of the Lamb in Revelation 7. When the mark of the beast is refused by Christians in Revelation 13, the result is economic persecution for Christians, for they are unable to buy or sell without this mark. This imagery can readily apply to any contemporary business situation, such as when an employee refuses to cooperate with unjust business practices and is liable to losing his or her job.

The final verse of this vision shows the visionary signaling to readers that he is about to provide a clue in code, whose decipherment will require their wisdom. The code contains the number that provides the identity of the beast, the now infamous number 666. "This calls for wisdom: let him who has understanding reckon the number of the beast, for it is a human number, its number is six hundred and sixty-six" (Revelation 13:18).

Because the number is a code, there have been arguments throughout history about how to decipher it. The number 666 has been applied to infamous tyrants like Hitler, and even to leaders of competing religious denominations, as in some applications of 666 to the pope. The code number seems to be based on the numerical value of letters of the alphabet (which before the invention of Arabic numerals were used as numbers). If so, the most widely accepted scholarly decoding of the number 666 is the sum of the numerical values in the Hebrew letters for the name "Nero Caesar." This solution is especially appealing in light of Nero's persecution of Christians and of Revelation's previous mysterious references to the myths about Nero's resurrection (see Revelation 13:3, 12).

Conclusion

This is only a small sampling of theological readings of New Testament texts, with some inspiration from theological exegesis by early church fathers like Sts. Irenaeus and Athanasius. Several of these New Testament texts relate to Old Testament texts that we read in the preceding chapter. These interrelated examples can further validate recognition that the Scriptures are indeed a unity when they are read in faith as writings inspired by God. Biblical unity, however, does not depend principally on such intertextual interrelationships among Old and New Testament books as were featured in the last two chapters. The Bible's unity makes sense primarily in light of belief that God is the single primary author of every writing in both the Old and New Testaments.

The Bible is a unity because in it, God tells his own story of our creation and salvation. This story begins with God's decision to create the world and to place human beings in delegated dominion over material creation. God's plan was disturbed by the disobedience of Adam and the consequent alienation of all humans from their originally intended intimacy with their Creator. The rest of the biblical story narrates God's efforts to recall humanity to intimacy with him.

As St. Athanasius has demonstrated, the climax of God's biblical story is the incarnation, when God's Son took on human flesh and lived among us and shared our human condition and suffering and death. By taking on our human nature, God's Son made our story his own story as well. When the Son of God became Immanuel, "God with us," he personally joined us in our story. Accounts of Jesus walking the roads of Galilee with his followers make it easier to realize that Immanuel walks with each of us in our own life journeys through his Holy Spirit given to us in baptism. We yet await in faith and in hope the final chapter of God's story, when his Son, Jesus, will ultimately return from the Father's right hand in heaven "to judge the living and the dead, and his kingdom will have no end."

Notes

1. To emphasize his comparison between the first Adam and Christ (the second Adam), Paul here ignores the role of Eve in Genesis 3.

2. Hebrews 2:14-15: "Since therefore the children share in flesh and blood, he [Jesus] himself likewise partook of the same nature, that through death he might destroy him who has the power of death, that is, the devil, and deliver all those who through fear of death were subject to lifelong bondage."

3. Compare Psalm 34:20: "Many are the afflictions of the righteous; but the LORD delivers him out of them all. He keeps all his bones; not one of them is broken."

4. Chapter 21 has the appearance of an epilogue added to the gospel, which clarifies some misunderstandings about whether Jesus had foretold that the beloved disciple would not die, occasioned apparently by some Christians' shock when he unexpectedly died (John 21:20-24).

Peter turned and saw following them the disciple whom Jesus loved, who had lain close to his breast at the supper and had said, "Lord, who is it that is going to betray you?" When Peter saw him, he said to Jesus, "Lord, what about this man?" Jesus said to him, "If it is my will that he remain until I come, what is that to you? Follow me!" *The saying spread abroad among the brethren that this disciple was not to die; yet Jesus did not say to him that he was not to die,* but, "If it is my will that he remain until I come, what is that to you?" This is the disciple who is bearing witness to these things, and who has written these things; and we know that his testimony is true. (emphasis added)

5. Cf. Craig S. Keener and InterVarsity Press, *The IVP Bible Background Commentary: New Testament* (Downers Grove, IL: InterVarsity Press, 1993), commentary on Revelation 12:1: "Ancient writers sometimes meant signs in heaven astrologically, but these signs were also fairly common as props in apocalyptic visions. The sun, moon and twelve stars help identify the woman as the twelve tribes of Israel (Gen 37:9)." (accessed via Libronix digital library)

Jean-Louis D'Aragon, SJ, calls this section "the heart of the Apocalypse." He continues, "The power of evil, represented by a monster, is radically opposed to the Messiah and his people; filled with hatred, the devil spares no pains to destroy Christ and his Church (ch. 12). To fulfill his purpose, the dragon dominates the Beast and urges it on against the Church; this Beast is the Roman Empire, which demands that all men accord divine honor to the emperor (ch. 13)." [in Raymond E. Brown, Joseph A. Fitzmyer, and Roland Edmund Murphy, *The Jerome Biblical Commentary* (electronic ed.; Englewood Cliffs, NJ: Prentice Hall, 1968; Published in electronic form by Logos Research Systems, 1996, § 56 (C) "The Dragon and the Lamb" (12:1–14:20)].

A CONVERSATION ABOUT THE FUTURE OF CATHOLIC BIBLICAL SCHOLARSHIP

In 2002, Luke Timothy Johnson and I published an invitation to fellow Catholic biblicists to engage in an earnest conversation about the urgency for Catholic biblical scholarship to move beyond the narrowly academic and historical programmatic priorities of scholarship.[1] We recommended that Catholic scholars refocus our approaches more intensively on the Bible as God's word and on apportioning a greater percentage of our scholarly efforts toward interpreting Scripture in explicit service of the Catholic Church and its theology, worship, and living. One objective of our book was to address the relatively greater scholarly neglect of Vatican II's second mandate, "to read Scripture in the Spirit in which it was written" (*Dei Verbum* § 12 and *Catechism of the Catholic Church* § 112–14).

The publication of our book sparked a considerable number of reviews and responses, many lengthy, and some negative and even heated. The majority, however, were primarily positive and receptive to its major concerns, though frequently including assorted cautions. At the University of Chicago on April 26, 2003, the Lumen Christi Institute held a colloquium in which scholars Gary Anderson, Carolyn Osiek, and Paul Griffiths provided spirited responses to updated assessments by co-authors Johnson and myself on our book and the concerns it raised.[2]

Most recently, the winter 2006 issue of the theological journal *Nova et Vetera* featured a symposium of five written responses to our book, three by Catholics and two by Protestants.[3] We original co-authors wrote independent replies to the five respondents, preferring not to consult each other on how each would answer the sometimes forceful criticisms or challenges raised.

The three Catholic responses all confirmed the book's fundamental request for more explicitly theological perspectives and Catholic concerns in doing and applying biblical scholarship. They concentrated primarily on moving the conversation forward into new areas or applications. Former Catholic Biblical Association president Frank Matera emphasized "balance and proportion" in implementing a more consciously theological approach to Catholic biblical scholarship.[4] He encouraged balance and proportion in exegesis between history and theology, between *the* (overall) theology and multiple theologies of the Bible, between Old and New Testaments, and between the ecclesial (church) and academic dimensions of exegesis. In the light of Luke Johnson's caution against seeking a single theology of the Bible or even of the Old or New Testament, a different expression might be more apt. Perhaps an alternative to "*the* theology" of Scripture or to "*the* theology" of the Old or New Testament might be a balance between what patristic authors referred to as the "underlying message" or "overarching biblical narrative" of creation and salvation in Scripture (understood in faith as a unified revelation from its primary author, God) and the multiple theologies and perspectives of individual biblical writings and authors.

Stephen D. Ryan, OP, Old Testament professor at the Dominican House of Studies in Washington, DC, and Oliver-Thomas

Venard, OP, New Testament professor at the École Biblique in Jerusalem, both moved the conversation forward into topics beyond those featured in our book. Ryan discussed implications for theories of inspiration of competing textual traditions of some Old Testament writings. Venard described how the next generation of Catholic biblical scholars was producing a replacement for the Jerusalem Bible in a radically reconceived format that has similarities to the Talmud, the ancient Jewish commentary that cited rabbinical commentaries, reception, and application of the biblical passages, alongside the quoted Scriptures. The new format would put greatly increased emphasis on Catholic reception of the Bible—that is, on how the church has received each book of Scripture in its life, worship, theology, and even art.

The two Protestant contributions, which were the most sharply critical, have been the most productive for my own further investigation of the issues raised in our book. Richard Hays, New Testament professor at Duke, has been independently engaged for some time in parallel scholarly concerns to develop and apply theological (and ethical) interpretations of Scripture.[5] In fact, the volume he co-edited with Ellen Davis the year after our book appeared can function as a complementary volume, and its "Nine Theses on the Interpretation of Scripture" closely parallel the aspects of pre-critical theological exegesis recommended by Luke Johnson in our book.[6]

Although the contribution by Professor David Yeago mentioned several criticisms of our positions similar to those by Hays, his positive suggestions proved to be the most immediate assistance toward my further research and writing on theological exegesis. Yeago was a most helpful guide to how the patristic writers can model ways that we today can recover more explicitly theological readings of Scripture.[7] He most constructively pointed to other scholarly writings that have promoted theological biblical interpretation and discriminating recovery of insights and approaches from patristic interpretation. Most of these writings were being produced during or after the writing of our book.[8] One of Yeago's own articles has proven to be especially fertile for my learning how to read Scripture theologically from Fathers of the Church like St. Athanasius.[9]

One of my most encouraging discoveries in the years after the publication of *The Future of Catholic Biblical Scholarship* has been my realization of how many theological scholars specializing in Scripture, in history of theology, and in systematic and moral theology have concerns similar to ours and are working energetically toward developing a viable contemporary theological interpretation of Scripture. Here at Marquette University, I have found colleagues specializing in Scripture and in patristic, medieval, and Byzantine theology, in addition to systematic and moral theologians, as well as graduate students, who are avidly studying fathers like Sts. Irenaeus and Athanasius and medieval theologians like St. Thomas Aquinas, and finding in them guides to theological interpretation of Scripture. In addition, many scholars are gathering in seminars or task forces devoted to theological and spiritual biblical interpretation at national and international biblical and theological conferences, such as at the Catholic Biblical Association and the Fellowship of Catholic Scholars.

Increasing numbers of new books, manuscripts being prepared for publication, and dissertations are being devoted to developing and exemplifying such theological interpretation inspired and guided by patristic and medieval (and post-Reformation) biblical interpreters. I have become convinced that religiously motivated Christian and Jewish scholars are entering a new phase of biblical interpretation, one that emphasizes theological exegesis and interpretation. This new phase is building on, but promises to transcend the limitations of, earlier historical and literary critical phases of biblical scholarship. I am quite hopeful that we will soon witness many transforming repercussions of the double mandate of *Dei Verbum* at Vatican II for the faith and life of the church and believers.

Notes

1. Luke Timothy Johnson and William S. Kurz, SJ, *The Future of Catholic Biblical Scholarship: A Constructive Conversation* (Grand Rapids, MI: Wm. B. Eerdmans, 2002).

2. See Luke Timothy Johnson's brief account of this colloquium in his response, "Conversation, Conversion, and Construction," in "Book Symposium: Luke Timothy Johnson and William S. Kurz, SJ, *The Future of Catholic Biblical Scholarship*," in *Nova et Vetera* Vol. 4, No. 1 (Winter 2006) 95–200: pp. 172–85, at 172. Subsequent references to symposium articles refer to pages in this journal volume.

3. "Book Symposium: Luke Timothy Johnson and William S. Kurz, SJ, *The Future of Catholic Biblical Scholarship*," in *Nova et Vetera* Vol. 4, No. 1 (Winter 2006) 95–200.

4. Frank J. Matera, "The Future of Catholic Biblical Scholarship: Balance and Proportion," in "Book Symposium" in *Nova et Vetera* 4:1, 120–32.

5. In his response to our book, Hays refers to the ecumenical colloquium, Duke University's "Scripture Project," which discussed and recommended how to make biblical scholarship more theological and of greater service to the church. Some of his most severe criticisms of both Johnson and me flowed from his observable pain at our failure to appreciate how close his concerns, methods, and often even conclusions about theological interpretation as a Wesleyan were to our proposals as Catholics (Richard B. Hays, "The Future of Christian Bibli-

cal Scholarship," 95–120 in the *Nova et Vetera* 2006 symposium).

6. Ellen F. Davis and Richard B. Hays, eds., "Nine Theses on the Interpretation of Scripture," *The Art of Reading Scripture* (Grand Rapids, MI: Wm. B. Eerdmans, 2003), 1–5. Simply listing the nine theses can illustrate how parallel and complementary are the proposals of the Scripture Project with Johnson's list:

1. Scripture truthfully tells the story of God's action of creating, judging, and saving the world.

2. Scripture is rightly understood in light of the church's rule of faith as a coherent dramatic structure.

3. Faithful interpretation of Scripture requires an engagement with the entire narrative: the New Testament cannot be rightly understood apart from the Old, nor can the Old be rightly understood apart from the New.

4. Texts of Scripture do not have a single meaning limited to the intent of the original author. In accord with Jewish and Christian traditions, we affirm that Scripture has multiple complex senses given by God, the author of the whole drama.

5. The four canonical gospels narrate the truth about Jesus.

6. Faithful interpretation of Scripture invites and presupposes participation in the community brought into being by God's redemptive action—the church.

7. The saints of the church provide guidance in how to interpret and perform Scripture.

8. Christians need to read the Bible in dialogue with diverse others outside the church.

9. We live in the tension between the "already" and the "not yet" of the kingdom of God; consequently, Scripture calls the church to ongoing discernment, to continually fresh rereadings of the text in the light of the Holy Spirit's ongoing work in the world.

7. David S. Yeago, "Re-Entering the Scriptural World," 159–71 in the *Nova et Vetera* symposium on our book.

8. For example, Yeago alerted me to a most recent book by John J. O'Keefe and R. R. Reno, *Sanctified Vision: An Introduction to Early Christian Interpretation of the Bible* (Baltimore: Johns Hopkins University Press, 2005). It provides an extraordinarily helpful introduction to patristic interpretation. Also quite profitable was Yeago's recommendation of Christopher R. Seitz, *Figured*

Out: Typology and Providence in Christian Scripture (Louisville: Westminster John Knox, 2001).

9. David S. Yeago, "The New Testament and the Nicene Dogma: A Contribution to the Recovery of Theological Exegesis," in Stephen E. Fowl, ed. *The Theological Interpretation of Scripture: Classic and Contemporary Readings* (Malden, MA: Blackwell, 1997) pp. 87–100.

Also from The Word Among Us Press

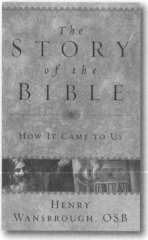

Item# BBIBE6

The Story of the Bible
How It Came to Us
Fr. Henry Wansbrough, OSB

Why did a number of early gospels, like the Gospel of Judas, never make it into the canon of Scripture? What is the *true* story of the Bible? A leading international Scripture scholar, Fr. Henry Wansbrough, OSB, provides the answers to these questions and many more in this balanced, fast-paced, and entertaining account.

140 pages, 5⅜ x 8½, softcover.

To order call 1-800-775-9673
or order online at www.wordamongus.org